THE
DECISION-MAKING
BLUEPRINT

A SIMPLE GUIDE TO
BETTER CHOICES
IN LIFE AND WORK

PATRIK EDBLAD

Disclaimer

Please note that this book is for entertainment purposes only. The views expressed are those of the author alone and should not be taken as expert instruction or commands. The reader is responsible for his or her actions.

ISBN-13: 978-1-942761-98-3

YOUR FREE BONUS BUNDLE

We'll be covering a lot of powerful concepts in this book. To make it as easy as possible for you to internalize them and use them in your decision-making, this companion resource contains:

- 3 beautiful posters that outline all the cognitive biases, logical fallacies, and mental models covered in the book.
- 45 handy flash cards to help you learn all these concepts by heart.
- A simple checklist of mental models for you to use every time you make an important decision.

Go here to grab *The Decision-Making Blueprint Bonus Bundle*
PatrikEdblad.com/the-decision-making-blueprint-book-bonuses

GET THE GOOD LIFE BLUEPRINT AUDIO SERIES
FOR FREE

If you enjoy listening to audiobooks, I have great news for you! You can get the entire audio version of *The Good Life Blueprint Series* for FREE by signing up for a 30-day Audible trial.

Go here to get started:

https://geni.us/Edblad-TGLB-Audible

CONTENTS

PART 1: INTRODUCTION

You cannot change your destination overnight,
but you can change direction overnight.

—Jim Rohn

The Secrets to Great Decision-Making

Throughout history, standard economic theory was dominated by the model of "homo economicus": the economic man. According to that model, humans are self-interested, intelligent, and analytical beings who can control their feelings and impulses. The economic man constantly evaluates all the facts, weighs the costs and benefits, and makes rational decisions to maximize personal well-being.

This view of humans as cold and rational calculators provides a convenient foundation for economic theories.

The only problem? No such person exists.

The Fall of Homo Economicus

It turns out that people often make decisions that don't deliver the best outcomes. Sometimes, we even make choices that we know will hurt our future prospects.

The first researchers to study these peculiar tendencies extensively were psychologists Daniel Kahneman and Amos Tversky. In the early 1970s, they started investigating the psychology involved in decision-making and running experiments to test their hypotheses.

Over the coming years, they compiled a long list of well-documented irrational behaviors, and in 1979 they published their key paper, "Prospect Theory: An Analysis of Decision Under Risk."[1]

Their findings caused a lot of controversy, especially among economists looking to protect their worldview. But Kahneman and Tversky stood their ground, and their work eventually marked the start for a new field of study.

The Rise of Behavioral Economics

Behavioral economics is a subfield of economics that studies how psychological, social, and emotional factors influence decision-making. The fundamental principle of this discipline is that people make systematic errors in their thinking.

Behavioral economists have found that the vast majority of our choices aren't the result of careful calculations. Instead, we rely heavily on mental shortcuts like rules of thumb, intuition, and common sense to form judgments, solve problems, and make decisions.

These shortcuts can work well in a lot of situations but, at times, they also result in cognitive biases and logical fallacies, thinking errors that distort our reasoning and derail our judgment.

An Ancient Brain in a Modern World

So, why do we make systematic errors in our thinking? Why do we use mental shortcuts instead of carefully calculating our decisions? What makes us susceptible to biases and fallacies?

The answers to those questions lie in our evolutionary past. Our brains have evolved for millions of years, not to maximize our well-being, but to keep us alive.

For most of our history, we lived in an environment that was wildly different from modern society. And that explains why we reason the way we do.

Mental shortcuts provided an efficient means for us to make quick decisions with limited knowledge in a complex world.

A lot of decisions that seem irrational today served us well in the environment we evolved in. To illustrate that, let's have a look at an example.

Loss Aversion

People have a tendency to prefer avoiding losses to acquiring equivalent gains. In other words, we feel better not losing $10 than we do finding $10.

Some research suggests that losses are twice as powerful, psychologically, as gains. And from an evolutionary perspective, that's a useful mechanism.

For most of human history, reductions in resources could lead to death. In that scenario, it makes sense to place a higher value on preventing losses than obtaining gains.

In modern-day life, however, losses rarely have the same dire consequences. And since that's the case, loss aversion no longer makes rational sense.

In the past, loss aversion helped our ancestors protect their scarce resources and stay alive. But in the present, the same bias often leads to poor decisions. When investing, for example, most people keep losing stocks and sell winning stocks even though, rationally, they should do the exact opposite.

Bad Decisions Everywhere

Loss aversion is just one example of how the brain makes systematic errors. There are many other biases and fallacies that diminish our ability to make sound judgments and reason logically.

We are fundamentally wired for mistakes and, as a result, we make a lot of poor decisions. The evidence is everywhere.

Career choices, for instance, are often regretted or abandoned. According to a Gallup report,[2] a majority of Americans would change at least one education decision, including their choice of college, their major, or their degree, if they could do it all over again.

When it comes to our health, we consistently make choices that are bad for us. One in three adults doesn't get enough sleep.[3] Roughly the same number of people are physically inactive.[4] And out of all deaths worldwide, 20 percent are attributable to bad food choices.[5]

We don't do much better in our social lives. Young people frequently start relationships with people who are bad for them. About 40 to 50 percent of marriages end in divorce.[6] And at the end of life, some of the most common regrets are working too much and losing touch with friends.[7]

The reason we struggle so much in these areas, and many others, is that we lack decision-making skills. Despite the vast implications our choices have on our lives, we're never explicitly taught how to make them.

A Simple Guide to Great Thinking

The good news is that you can train your brain to think in new and better ways. And in this book, I will show you exactly how to do that. In the chapters ahead, you'll discover:

- The cognitive biases that distort your thinking, and how to counteract them.
- The logical fallacies that derail your judgment, and how to prevent them.
- The mental models you need to equip your mind with to make great decisions.

We'll draw from philosophical ideas, psychological research, and powerful concepts from a wide variety of disciplines so you can deeply understand and consistently improve the cognitive apparatus of your mind.

By the end of this book, you'll have a solid foundation for rational, logical, and effective thinking. As a result, you'll make smarter decisions and get better outcomes than ever before.

And if any of this sounds complicated—don't worry. Everything is explained in a clear and simple way. I'll take your hand and guide you every step of the way. All you have to do is follow along, absorb, and apply the concepts to your own thinking.

Your Decisions Shape Your Life

Each day, from the instant you wake up until the moment you fall asleep, you are making countless choices.

Some decisions are big: "What career should I pursue?," "Where should I live?," "Should I get married or not?" These choices are defining moments we know will have a significant impact on our lives.

Most decisions are small: "Should I get up or hit the snooze button?," "What should I have for lunch?," "Should I take the stairs or the elevator?" These choices might not matter much in the moment, but over time, they will compound into striking results.

So, to get desirable outcomes in life, you need to make good decisions—both big and small. Good decisions repeated over time lead to success. Bad decisions repeated over time lead to failure.

The choices you've made until now have brought you where you are right now. And the decisions you make going forward will determine the life you'll lead in the future.

Change Your Trajectory

If you read and implement what you learn in this book, I promise that you'll radically improve your decision-making skills.

You'll be able to spot the inherent mental errors and reasoning flaws in your mind. And you'll be able to use a wide variety of thinking tools to understand reality and solve problems.

In short, you'll think better. And that will allow you to experience the satisfaction of making great decisions and, ultimately, the fulfillment of shaping the life you want.

So, make a life-changing decision right now and keep on reading. Your future self will be happy you did.

On the next page, we'll have a quick look at how to best use this book. Then we'll get right into the good stuff as I lay out the Decision-Making Blueprint.

Let's dive in!

How to Use This Book

The Decision-Making Blueprint is divided into five parts. Right now you're reading part 1, which is the introduction. Next, in part 2, we'll examine the cognitive biases that distort your thinking and how to counteract them. Then, in part 3, we'll explore the logical fallacies that derail your judgment and how to prevent them. After that, in part 4, we'll equip your mind with the mental models you need to make great decisions. And lastly, in part 5, I'll share some final words on how to improve your decision-making skills continuously.

This book contains everything you need to improve your thinking, make smarter decisions, and get better results. But that will only happen if you move from theory to practice. So, commit right now to using the concepts in your everyday life right away.

As you're making choices, reflect on the cognitive biases that might influence your thinking. When you're talking to others, pay attention to the logical fallacies that show up. And whenever you're making an important decision, use the mental models at your disposal.

To make all of that as easy as possible, I recommend you download The Decision-Making Blueprint Bonus Bundle. The posters, flash cards, and checklist will make everything you're learning much simpler to internalize and put to use.

Are you ready? Let's get started!

PART 2: COGNITIVE BIASES

The mind of man at one and the same time is both the glory and the shame of the universe.

—Blaise Pascal

The Mental Errors That Distort Your Thinking

It's been estimated that the human brain can make roughly a billion billion calculations per second. That's far more than any computer that exists today.

In fact, it took one of the world's most powerful supercomputers—housing 705,024 processor cores and 1.4 million gigabytes of RAM—40 minutes to simulate just one second of thinking.[8]

But despite its impressive capacity, the brain still makes systematic mistakes.

Cognitive Biases

We all have inherent thinking errors in the way we perceive, process, and interpret information from the world around us.

Psychologists refer to these errors as cognitive biases: "a systematic pattern of deviation from norm or rationality in judgment."[9]

The world is an extremely complicated place, and cognitive biases are often a result of your brain's attempt to simplify the input it's receiving. And that's not necessarily a bad thing. Cognitive biases help us act fast, filter information, construct meaning, and remember what's important.

But they can also be problematic. At times, they lead to perceptual distortions, inaccurate judgment, and irrational decisions.

A fascinating study by researchers Eric Johnson and Daniel Goldstein[10] provides a great example of how cognitive bias can affect our choices—without us even realizing it. Let's have a look at it next.

Would You Like to Be an Organ Donor?

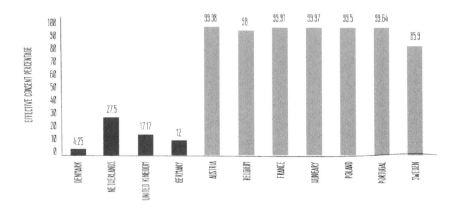

EFFECTIVE CONSENT RATES, BY COUNTRY. EXPLICIT CONSENT (OPT-IN, GOLD) AND PRESUMED CONSENT (OPT-OUT, BLUE)

This graph shows the percentage of people across several European countries who are willing to donate their organs after they die.

Note the massive difference between the countries on the left and the ones on the right. Why do you think that is?

At first glance, you might assume some major underlying factor like culture or religion caused these results, but at a closer look, that doesn't hold up.

Denmark and Sweden, the Netherlands and Belgium, Austria and Germany—these are all countries with similar cultures and religious beliefs.

Still, their organ donation percentages are wildly different. What's really going on here?

The Default Effect

What explains the differences between the countries is the design of the form related to organ donations in each region.

In the countries where the form has an "opt-in" design (i.e., "Check this box if you want to donate your organs"), people tend not to check the box.

And in the countries where the form has an "opt-out" design (i.e., "Check this box if you don't want to donate your organs"), people also tend not to check the box.

No matter which one of these forms people are presented with, an overwhelming majority of them will choose the default option.

When you decide whether to donate your organs, you may feel like you're making a deliberate choice. But in reality, you're much more likely to choose whatever is presented as the standard choice.

This is known as the default effect, and it's just one example of how cognitive biases can affect our decisions. In the upcoming pages, we'll cover many more.

Debiasing

It's important to note that you can't completely rid yourself of cognitive biases. That's not possible, nor desirable. As we've seen, cognitive biases have evolved for a reason. They are hardwired into your brain because you need them to navigate the world.

But what you can do is use debiasing to reduce the influence of biases in your judgment and decisions. That can be very helpful, especially when it comes to particularly important decisions.

So, in the chapters ahead, we'll look at the most common cognitive biases related to decision-making and what you can do to decrease their effects.

And we'll begin with the granddaddy of them all...

1. Confirmation Bias

Our tendency to favor information that
confirms our existing beliefs.

Imagine that you're participating in a psychology experiment. The experimenter gives you a three number sequence and informs you that these numbers follow a particular rule only she knows about.

Your task is to figure out what that rule is, and you can do that by proposing your own three number strings and asking the experimenter whether or not they meet the rule. The series of numbers you're given is:

2-4-6

Try it! What underlying rule do you think these numbers follow? And what's another string you can give to the experimenter to see if you're right?

If you're like most people, you'll assume the rule is "numbers increasing by two" or "ascending even numbers." To find out if you're right, you guess something like:

10-12-14

And to your delight, the experimenter says, "Yes, that string of numbers follows the rule." To make sure that your hypothesis is correct, you propose another sequence:

50-52-54

"Yes!" the experimenter says, and you confidently make your guess about the underlying rule: "Even numbers, ascending in twos!" To your surprise, the experimenter says "No!"

It turns out that the rule is "any ascending numbers." So, 10-12-14 and 50-52-54 fit the rule, but so does 1-2-3 or 9-748-1047.

The only way to figure that out is to guess strings of numbers that would prove your beloved hypothesis wrong—and that's not something that comes naturally to us. In the original study,[11] only one in five participants guessed the correct rule.

The 2-4-6 task beautifully illustrates our bias toward confirming, rather than disproving, our ideas. And that tendency has a massive influence on how we interpret information, form beliefs, and make decisions.

Consider, for example, the global warming controversy. Let's say Mary believes climate change is a serious issue. Because of that, she seeks out and reads stories about how the climate is changing. As a result, she continues to confirm and support those beliefs.

Meanwhile, Linda does not believe that climate change is a serious issue. Because of that, she seeks out and reads stories about how climate change is a hoax. As a result, she continues to confirm and support those beliefs instead.

The confirmation bias makes us pay attention to what supports our views and dismiss what doesn't. And the more convinced we become about something, the more we'll filter out and ignore all evidence to the contrary.

It feels much better to support our beliefs than it does to discredit them. Evaluating and adjusting our worldview is scary, uncomfortable, and strenuous. So we prefer strengthening it instead.

The confirmation bias helps us do that. But it does so at the expense of clear judgment. To keep an open, flexible, and rational mind, you have to continually challenge what you think you know.

You need to deliberately seek out disconfirming evidence and always be ready to change your mind. It's not easy but, with practice, it will make you much better at interpreting information, updating your beliefs, and making well-informed decisions.

2. Self-Serving Bias

*Our tendency to take credit for successes
and deny responsibility for failures.*

"If it worked, it was because of me. If it didn't, it was because of someone or something else." This kind of reasoning takes place all the time and, on a psychological level, it makes sense. We all feel a need to protect and build our self-esteem, and the self-serving bias helps us do that.

Imagine, for example, that you're trying to get your driver's license. If you pass your driving test on the first try, you'll probably think it happened because of your excellent driving skills. But if you fail, you'll likely blame it on the incompetent examiner, the awful car, the bad weather or, well, pretty much anything else other than your own performance.

Studies on the self-serving bias have found that it shows up in a wide variety of situations, including:

- School–If a student gets a good grade, it's because of his hard work and intelligence. But if he gets a bad grade, it's because of the poor teacher or the unfair test.[12]

- Work–If a job applicant gets hired, it's because of her qualifications. But if she doesn't, it's because the interviewer didn't like her.[13]

- Sports–If a team wins a game, it's because of practice and skill. But if they lose, it's because of the referee.[14]

We also consistently make what psychologists refer to as the "fundamental attribution error." When other people make mistakes, we blame the person. But when we make mistakes ourselves, we blame the circumstances.

Let's say you've gotten your driver's license (thanks to your excellent driving skills, of course), and you're cruising down the highway when, suddenly, somebody passes you going well over the speed limit. In this scenario, you'll likely conclude that the other driver is a reckless jerk.

But if the roles were reversed, and you're the one driving too fast, you'd probably blame the circumstances instead. Unlike other drivers, you're not some irresponsible maniac. If you're speeding, it's because the situation, perhaps an emergency, warranted it.

With these tendencies in mind, it's no surprise we also rate ourselves more positively than others. Research on what psychologists call "illusory superiority" shows that most of us consider ourselves better than average in school, at work, in social settings, and in many other situations.

Reasoning this way feels good. It helps us save face, hang on to our self-esteem, and avoid hurtful emotions like shame. But it also prevents our learning and growth. If you blame your failures on the circumstances, there's not much you can do about it. But if you accept responsibility for them, you can improve and do better next time.

So be mindful of your tendency to irrationally protect your self-esteem. When you experience setbacks, resist the urge to pass the blame and take ownership instead. Don't ask "Whose fault is this?" but "What can I learn from this?" That way, you can continually course-correct, make wiser decisions, and get better results.

3. Availability Bias

Our tendency to base our judgments on
what most easily springs to mind.

If you're like most people, you consume the morning news with a sense of anxiety and fear. Each day, we read about shootings, war, and the spread of nuclear weapons. It's no wonder most of us feel like the world is getting increasingly worse.

But the truth is that we are actually living in the least violent time in history. In his book *The Better Angels of Our Nature*,[15] psychologist Steven Pinker shows that the numbers of homicides, armed conflicts, and nuclear weapons are all actually declining.

Most people have a hard time accepting these statistics. Some even refuse to believe them. If this is the most peaceful time in history, then why are there so many reports of murders? Why does everyone keep talking about wars? And why do we hear about nuclear weapons all the time?

The answer is that we are living in the most reported time in history. Information about horrifying stories from all over the world is more easily accessible than ever before. So, while the likelihood of dangerous events is going down, the chance that you'll hear about them is going up.

And this is where the availability bias comes into play. When an event springs easily to mind, our brain will exaggerate the frequency and magnitude of it. We constantly overestimate the impact of stuff we remember and underestimate the things we don't hear about. In the words of Daniel Kahneman:

"People tend to assess the relative importance of issues by the ease with which they are retrieved from memory—and this is largely determined by the extent of coverage in the media."[16]

The availability bias makes us bad at assessing risks and estimating probabilities. And that, in turn, affects our feelings, decisions, and outcomes. For example:

- If we hear about a plane crash, we might develop a fear of flying that severely limits the places we can travel.

- If we're told about a shark attack, we might avoid the ocean every time we're at the beach.

- If someone in our neighborhood wins the lottery, we might waste a lot of money on tickets.

The chances of experiencing a plane crash, getting attacked by a shark, or winning the grand prize in a lottery are tiny. But the brain doesn't care about that. Instead, it bases its immediate judgments on the vividness of the stories we're told about these events.

To make well-informed decisions, you need to keep this tendency in mind. Whenever you're presented with news and stories, try to recall instances of the event that aren't so memorable. For example, ask yourself how many people you know who have:

- Not died in a plane crash?

- Never been attacked by a shark?

- Failed to win the lottery jackpot?

Or do a quick Google search and look up the real-world probabilities for these events. That way, you can keep the availability bias in check, minimize unnecessary stress, and avoid irrational decisions.

4. Survivorship Bias

*Our tendency to focus on things that "survive" a
process while overlooking those that don't.*

During World War II, the British military was losing their bombers at an alarming rate. As they were flying over enemy territory, they were being shot down so often that they decided to add armor to their planes.

But they couldn't shield the entire surface of their aircraft. That would make them too heavy to take off. So they decided to put the armor in the most critical places.

To find out what those areas were, they carefully investigated the aircraft that came back from battle and noted where they had been damaged the most. The investigators found that the majority of the bullet holes were on the wings, around the tail gunner, and down the center of the body.

Now, let's imagine that you were in charge of the investigation. With that information at your disposal, where would you put the armor?

Most likely, you would want to do what the real commanders planned on doing. They wanted to shield the parts that had the most bullet holes: the wings, the tail gunner, and the center of the body.

It seems like the obvious choice, but it would have been a terrible idea. Why? Remember, the investigators had only considered the aircrafts that *survived* their missions. None of the planes that had been shot down had been taken into account.

The holes in the examined aircraft represented the areas where the bombers could take damage and still make it home. Counterintuitively, it was the unharmed parts of the examined planes that needed the armor. Because if those were hit, the aircraft would be lost, and it wouldn't show up in the investigation.

Luckily for the British military, statistician Abraham Wald pointed that out and helped them avoid a crucial mistake.[17] But in everyday life, we fall for the survivorship bias all the time, and it has significant implications on our judgment and decisions.

Consider, for example, the famous stories of how successful people like Richard Branson, Bill Gates, and Mark Zuckerberg all dropped out of school. Learning about them, many people conclude that you don't need a college education to succeed.

But for every Branson, Gates, and Zuckerberg, there are thousands, if not millions, of other entrepreneurs who dropped out of school and failed in business. We just don't hear about them, and so we don't take them into account.

When you pay attention to the winners and ignore the losers, it's difficult to say if a particular strategy will be successful. So whenever you're presented with a success story, ask yourself if it provides a complete picture, or if it's only taking survivors into account. That way, you'll make more accurate judgments and avoid costly mistakes.

5. Loss Aversion

Our tendency to prefer avoiding losses
to acquiring equivalent gains.

Imagine that I invite you to play a game right now. The rules are simple. We'll flip a coin. If it shows heads, you'll lose $100. And if it shows tails, you'll win $100. Would you take that bet?

If you're like most people, you wouldn't. And since the risk and reward of the bet are precisely the same, that makes sense. So, let's change the rules a little. If it shows heads, you'll still lose $100. But if it shows tails, you'll now win $110. Would you take the bet this time?

Interestingly, most people would still not want to play. The game has a positive expected value of 10 percent, meaning that, on average, you'll win $10 every time you play. But that doesn't matter. Psychologically, the risk of losing our hard-earned $100 outweighs the potential reward.

Sure, we enjoy winning. But we really, really hate losing. And that leads to poor reasoning and silly decisions.

In fact, when researchers offer people the chance to play the coin flip game, they find that most of us demand a chance to win $200 or more to participate. And that, in the words of Daniel Kahneman, is "ridiculously loss averse."[18]

A major implication of loss aversion is something called the "endowment effect," our tendency to perceive things as more valuable just because we own them. To understand how it works, let's have a look at another experiment.

In this study,[19] the researchers took a big group of students and split them into two groups. They gave the first group a mug and asked, "For how much would you sell your mug?" and "How much would you pay for a candy bar?" Then they gave the second group a candy bar and asked, "For how much would you sell your candy bar?" and "How much would you pay for a mug?"

Since they gave out the mugs and candy randomly, you would expect that many people would prefer the other item. But that's not at all the case. What you'll find when you do this experiment is that almost no one switches.

The people who get mugs suddenly think mugs are amazing. And the people who get candy bars now think candy is terrific. Both groups end up valuing their item more highly and sticking to what they already have.

Loss aversion and the endowment effect makes us overprotect and overvalue what we have. And that often lead to choices, big and small, that are not in our best interest. It can make you hang on to losing stocks that ruin your portfolio, and it can make you keep needless possessions that clutter your house.

So whenever you feel anxious about a potential loss, compare the downside to the upside. Then dare to make the decision that makes rational sense, even if it feels uncomfortable. Over the long run, that will lead to much better results.

6. Status Quo Bias

Our tendency to prefer that things stay as they already are.

In the early 1980s, Coca-Cola was on the edge of losing the cola war to their rivals Pepsi. The previous fifteen years, Coke's market share had remained flat while Pepsi's climbed steadily. To make matters worse, more and more consumers were switching to diet soft drinks and non-cola beverages.

So Coca-Cola decided to do something drastic. They started experimenting with their original formula. A new recipe was put forth, and it seemed very promising. Blind taste tests showed people liked the new formula more than regular Coke *and* Pepsi by a large margin.

In 1985, they launched the new and improved version of their drink. But despite the test results, the response from the public was extremely negative. After being bombarded by phone calls, 40,000 letters, and tons of bad press, the company reintroduced its original formula within three months.

Interestingly, the return of "Coca-Cola Classic" resulted in a significant increase in sales. That made some people speculate that introducing the new formula was a marketing ploy to stimulate sales of the original drink. The Coca-Cola Company, however, maintains that it was a genuine attempt to replace the original product.

Regardless, the introduction of the new Coke recipe is an excellent example of the status quo bias.[20] We like things the way they already are, so we treat any changes to the current state of affairs with a lot of skepticism and resistance.

That tendency can partly be explained by loss aversion and the endowment effect. We weigh the potential losses of switching from the status quo more heavily than the potential gains. But several other tendencies also contributes to the status quo bias, including:

- Psychological commitment–We want to justify previous actions and maintain a consistent self-image.

- Mere exposure–We prefer certain things just because they are familiar to us.

- Regret avoidance–We feel worse about bad decisions than we do about poor outcomes from inaction.

All of these tendencies can have big impacts on our decisions. Do you remember the organ donor study[21] a few chapters back? The status quo bias explains why people are inclined to stick with the default option. It's also why we tend to, for example:

- Go to the same restaurant, sit in the same spot, and order the same dish.

- Stick with the same internet, phone, and TV providers.

- Use the same bank, savings options, and insurance companies.

And there's nothing inherently wrong with any of those choices. In fact, the status quo bias can help us save energy and prevent unnecessary risks. But it can also make us miss out on great opportunities.

So whenever you feel like turning down a new choice, ask yourself why that is. Is your default option truly better, or are you being swayed by the comfort of the status quo?

7. Anchoring Bias

Our tendency to rely too much on an initial piece of information.

Imagine that you're out shopping, and as you walk into a clothing store, you spot a jacket you like. You try it on, check yourself out in the mirror, and decide you have to have it. Now, imagine the following two scenarios:

1) You check the price tag, and the jacket is $500. But a salesperson walks by and says, *"I'm sorry. That price is wrong. The jacket is really $300."*

2) You check the price tag, and the jacket is $100. But a salesperson walks by and says, *"I'm sorry. That price is wrong. The jacket is really $300."*

If you're like most people, you're much more likely to buy the jacket in the first scenario. But that doesn't really make sense, does it? After all, the price you'd have to pay is exactly the same in both scenarios. So why are we more comfortable buying the jacket in the first one?

The answer is what psychologists refer to as anchoring.[22] As soon as we've read the price tag, we'll use it as a reference point—an anchor—for everything that happens after that.

If the initial price was higher, we'll feel like we're getting a good deal. And if the initial price was lower, we'll feel like we're getting a bad deal.

Marketers are well aware of this bias and use it to their advantage all the time. Here are some examples of anchoring strategies often used in marketing:

- Original vs discounted price–Retailers often present the old price of a product next to the new, discounted price. This way, the old price acts as an anchor that makes the new price more appealing.

- Price perception manipulation–Car dealerships often place their most expensive cars at the front of their display rooms. Once you've walked past them, the cars in the back don't seem all that expensive.

- Purchase quantity limits–Stores sometimes use signs like "Limit: 12 per customer." The number 12 then acts as an anchor that makes customers buy more than they intended.

And anchoring doesn't just occur in purchasing decisions. There are many examples of anchoring in everyday life, such as:

- Teacher's judgments–In some schools, children are tracked and categorized by ability from an early age. Those categories then become anchors that shape the teacher's expectations for the children.

- Longevity assumptions–If your parents lived to be very old, you'll likely expect to live a long life, too. But if your parents died young, you'll probably be surprised if you live for a long time.

- First impressions–When you meet someone for the first time, that encounter becomes a reference point for all future interactions. It's unfortunate and unfair, but first impressions matter A LOT.

As you can see, the anchoring bias has a huge impact on our lives. As you draw conclusions, form judgments, and make decisions, keep this sneaky tendency in mind.

Ask yourself if you are giving adequate consideration to all the information available, or if you're giving undue weight to some prior reference point. That way, you'll avoid getting stuck to irrelevant and irrational anchors.

8. Hyperbolic Discounting

Our tendency to value smaller immediate rewards more than larger future rewards.

If you're like most people, you know very well what it's like to procrastinate. On more than one occasion, you've probably told yourself stuff like:

- "I should stick to my diet, but if I have a cupcake now, I can make up for it tomorrow."
- "I should go to the gym, but I really don't feel like it right now, so I'll get started Monday morning."
- "I should save more for retirement, but I want to buy a new phone, so I'll start saving next month."

Whenever you reason along these lines, you're falling victim to what behavioral economists call hyperbolic discounting.[23] It sounds complicated, but it just means that we value rewards differently at different points in time. In the short term, we're impatient and prefer immediate, smaller rewards. But in the long term, we're patient and prefer distant, bigger rewards.

A classic experiment[24] illustrates it well. When researchers offer people $100 today or $120 in a month, most people choose the $100. But if they offer people $100 in a year or $120 in a year and a month, suddenly, most people will wait the extra month to get the $120.

Even though the time and value difference are the exact same in both scenarios, we perceive them very differently. The further into the future a reward is, the more we tend to discount its value. So it's really no surprise that we consistently find ourselves procrastinating.

The short-term pleasures of eating a cupcake, taking a nap, or playing around with a new phone are immediate and tangible. Conversely, the long-term benefits of eating healthy, exercising, and saving money for retirement are far away and abstract.

That imbalance makes us choose short-term pleasures now while postponing long-term benefits for the future. A study on grocery-buying habits[25] demonstrates it nicely: when buying groceries online for delivery tomorrow, people buy a lot more ice cream and a lot fewer vegetables than when they're ordering for delivery next week.

The opposite of hyperbolic discounting is what psychologists call delayed gratification, the ability to resist smaller immediate rewards to receive larger future rewards.

Research links this ability with a host of positive life outcomes such as better grades, lower substance abuse rates, greater financial security, and improved physical and mental health.[26]

And it makes sense, doesn't it? No matter what goal you want to achieve, it almost always requires you to resist something easy and do something hard.

To be successful, you have to mitigate hyperbolic discounting so you can make wise choices in the moment and get better outcomes in the future.

We'll cover many ways to do that later on in this book but, for now, pay attention to effects that hyperbolic discounting is having on daily decision-making.

Consciously evaluate the tradeoff that you're making between the present and future, and try to make the best decision possible—even if it's uncomfortable.

If you regularly delay gratification, you'll become increasingly better at it. And your future self will be grateful for it.

9. Dunning-Kruger Effect

Our tendency to be more confident the less we know.

In 2005, I tried online poker for the first time. I learned the rules, deposited $30, and quickly doubled my money. There was no question in my mind—I was a natural at the game. So, I played again the next day... and quickly lost it all.

It wasn't until I started studying poker theory and strategy that I began to grasp the complexity of the game. I learned about pot odds, expected value, hand ranges, and many other concepts that I previously had been oblivious to.

The more I learned, the more I realized that I didn't understand. But my game kept improving. Eventually, I reached the point where I could play poker full time. And during those years, I noticed something interesting.

Beginners usually make every play with certainty, while experienced players question every decision. Bad players are confident, and good players doubtful. And that tendency doesn't just show up in poker but in any area of expertise.

In fact, it's so common that Bertrand Russell once stated, "The whole problem with the world is that fools and fanatics are always so certain of themselves, and wiser people so full of doubts."

And he's not alone; Socrates, William Shakespeare, Charles Darwin, and Friedrich Nietzsche have all commented on our propensity to be more confident the less we know.

But it wasn't until the late 1990s that this tendency was given a name. That's when social psychologists David Dunning and Justin Kruger did an experiment where they tested people's abilities in logical thinking, grammar, and sense of humor.

It turned out that those who performed the worst dramatically over-estimated their ability. And conversely, those who performed the best believed that they had in fact done poorly.

Dunning and Kruger reported their findings in an article called "Unskilled and unaware of it: how difficulties in recognizing one's own incompetence lead to inflated self-assessments,"[27] and the tendency came to be called the Dunning-Kruger effect.

According to David Dunning, "If you're incompetent, you can't know you're incompetent,"[28] and that has two major implications:

1) It leads to mistakes and poor decisions.
2) It prevents you from catching your errors.

In other words, not only does the Dunning-Kruger effect make you perform poorly, but it also makes it hard to recognize how badly you are in fact doing.

So, whenever you feel confident in a certain area of expertise, keep this tendency in mind. Remember that confidence might very well be a sign of invisible holes in your competence.

Be skeptical of your abilities, especially when you're a beginner. You'll make fewer mistakes, reach better decisions, and learn more from feedback.

10. Bias Blind Spot

*Our tendency to recognize biases in others
but fail to see them in ourselves.*

As you learn about the cognitive biases in this book, you'll probably notice that they show up frequently in everyday life:

- Maybe you're discussing politics with a friend, and you spot a strong confirmation bias in his views.

- Perhaps someone expresses worry for a terrorist attack, and you realize it's because of availability bias from watching the news.

- Someone might tell you about the great deal they got on their new TV, and you recognize that they've fallen for the anchoring bias.

It's certainly useful to be aware of the mental errors going on around you. But the real benefit lies in identifying these flaws in your own thinking. It's only when you recognize the limitations of your cognitive apparatus that you can improve it.

Unfortunately, it's much harder to spot biases in ourselves than in others. In fact, that tendency is itself a mental error known as the bias blind spot or the bias bias. Behavioral decision researcher Erin McCormick provides this explanation.[29]

"When physicians receive gifts from pharmaceutical companies, they may claim that the gifts do not affect their decisions about what medicine to prescribe because they have no memory of the gifts biasing their prescriptions. However, if you ask them whether a gift might unconsciously bias the decisions of other physicians, most will agree that other physicians are unconsciously biased by the gifts, while continuing to believe that their own decisions are not. This disparity is the bias blind spot, and occurs for everyone, for many different types of judgments and decisions."

What's particularly striking about this tendency is how widespread it is. A study by McCormick and her colleagues[30] found that out of 661 participants, only one claimed to be more biased than the average person. The other 99.8 percent rated themselves as less biased than other people. And that, of course, is statistically impossible.

So why do we assume that we are less biased than others? A lot of it ties back into the self-serving bias, illusory superiority, and our tendency to protect our self-esteem. We generally consider biases undesirable, so we like to think of ourselves as unbiased or, at least, less biased than average.

But there's nothing wrong with being biased. As we've learned earlier in this book, biases are hardwired into our brains because we need them to navigate the world. And denying their influence only gets you stuck in your old ways of thinking.

So if you're still thinking that you're probably less biased than others, remember where that thought comes from. That's right—it comes from your brain. And your brain is biased to think that it's not biased.

Let go of the intuition that your thinking is somehow immune. Accept that you are just as vulnerable to thinking errors as everyone else. It's counterintuitive, but it will open you up for sharper judgment, smarter decisions, and better results.

PART 3: LOGICAL FALLACIES

It has been said that man is a rational animal. All my life I have been searching for evidence which could support this.

—Bertrand Russell

The Reasoning Flaws That
Derail Your Judgment

Aristotle once described humans as "the rational animal." He claimed that rationality is our "distinguishing characteristic," the ability that sets us apart from all other animals.

Unlike other creatures, humans have the capacity to apply logic, establish facts, and make sense of things.

We do that by *reason*, and the process of doing so is called *reasoning*.

But just because we're capable of these things doesn't mean we're good at them.

Logical Fallacies

As we've seen in part 1 of the book, the brain is susceptible to cognitive biases—thinking errors in the way we process information.

On top of that, the brain doesn't appear to have evolved for precise logic. There are many reasoning traps that our minds fall into. These are called logical fallacies: "the modes in which, by neglecting the rules of logic, we often fall into erroneous reasoning."[31] Or, put simply: errors in reasoning.

Logical fallacies are like tricks or illusions of thought and, as such, they can often be difficult to spot. Let's, once again, use the organ donor study[32] as an example.

Swedish Organ Donors

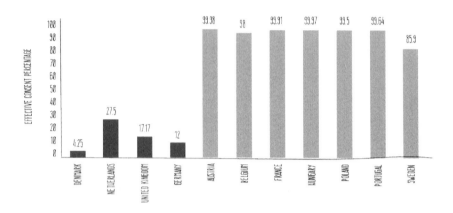

EFFECTIVE CONSENT RATES, BY COUNTRY. EXPLICIT CONSENT (OPT-IN, GOLD) AND PRESUMED CONSENT (OPT-OUT, BLUE)

Remember, this graph shows the percentage of people across several European countries who are willing to donate their organs after they die. This time note that Sweden, for whatever reason, has a slightly lower consent rate than the other countries on the right.

And now, let's imagine that you're in charge of increasing that number. How would you go about that?

One thing you could do is include a note on the organ donor form that says something like, "The vast majority of Swedes donate their organs."

That's a very persuasive statement that would probably convince a lot more people to donate. But, looking at it logically, it really shouldn't.

"Everybody's Doing It"

Donating your organs might very well be the right thing to do. But the fact that many people donate has nothing to do with it.

Just because something is popular, that doesn't make it the right decision. As we all know, a lot of people have been wrong about a lot of stuff a lot of times.

So if someone reads that "the vast majority of Swedes donate their organs" and chooses to donate based solely on that fact, they've fallen for a logical fallacy known as appeal to popularity.

And that's completely understandable. If something is popular, our common sense tells us it must also be good, true, or valid.

But that's not the case, and if we don't pay attention to logical pitfalls like this, they will cloud our judgment and create poor decisions.

Don't Be Fooled

By becoming aware of logical fallacies, you can identify and call out poor reasoning. You'll be able to examine information critically and adjust your decisions accordingly.

And that's an important skill, especially in a society where politicians, media, and marketers prey on logical fallacies to influence your decisions.

In the chapters ahead, we'll look at the most common logical fallacies relating to decision-making and how you can expose and prevent them.

And we'll begin with one I'm sure you've come across many times…

1. Hasty Generalization

Our tendency to draw conclusions based on small sample sizes.

Imagine I told you that the average height of all the people in the entire world is about 6.2 feet. And when you ask me how I learned that, I replied, "It was simple, really. I just measured myself."

After getting over the initial shock of my apparent stupidity, you'd probably inform me that I can't just measure myself and draw such a conclusion. I'd need a much larger sample size.

And, of course, you'd be right. In obvious examples like this, we have an intuitive sense for what statisticians call the law of large numbers,[33] which states, "As a sample size grows, its mean gets closer to the average of the whole population."

But there are many less clear-cut situations where we fail to take sample size into account. Consider, for example, this statement:

In a telephone poll of 300 seniors, 60 percent support the president.[34]

If you had to create a headline of three words to describe those findings, what would it be? If you're like most people, you'll write "Elderly Support President."

And those words do a good job of conveying the essence of the story. But the details of the poll design—that it was done over the phone with a sample of just 300—gets left out.

The takeaway? We pay much more attention to the *content* of messages than we do to the *reliability* of the information.

You've probably seen plenty of commercials where four out of five dentists recommend some toothpaste. That seems convincing, but only because we focus on the *content* of the message—authorities in the field think highly of the product.

If we instead turned our attention to the *reliability* of the information—the fact that we don't know the sample size—we'd come to a very different conclusion. After all, there's a good chance only five dentists were actually asked. And if you did a proper poll with a random sampling of 1000 dentists, perhaps only 20 percent would recommend the brand.

Accurate assumptions require sufficient sample sizes. But in everyday life, we often forget about that and, as a result, make hasty generalizations. Here are a few examples:

- Your dad smokes four packs of cigarettes per day and lives to be eighty years old. He's just one person, but you still conclude that smoking can't be that bad for you.

- You meet someone for the first time, and he makes a bad impression on you. It's just one meeting, but you still assume that he's a rude person.

- You try investing in the stock market and lose half of the money spent in your first week. It's a short period of time, but you still conclude the stock market isn't for you.

As you can see, hasty generalizations often lead to inaccurate conclusions, bad judgments, and poor decisions. So always pay attention to the reliability of information. When the sample size is small, suspend your judgment and try to find more reliable data.

2. False Cause

Our tendency to presume that one thing caused another.

Imagine that it's a sunny day at the beach. It's terribly hot, so you decide to cool off in the ocean. As you make your way to the shoreline, you spot an ice cream stand.

Before you decide whether or not to treat yourself, consider the following statistical fact: when sales of ice cream go up, so do deaths by drowning. How should that information affect your decision?

If you're like most people, you'll assume that having ice cream before going into the water is dangerous. But it's really not, and to understand why, we need to recognize the difference between correlation and causation.

Correlation means that there is a relationship between two things. Causation means that one thing causes another thing to happen.

A correlation between two things doesn't necessarily mean there is causation between the two. So the fact that there is a relationship between ice cream sales and deaths by drowning doesn't mean that ice cream causes drowning.

Instead, the correlation depends on a third factor: temperature. When it's hot outside, people buy more ice cream. They're also more likely to go swimming, which increases the number of drownings. So, ice cream sales and deaths by drowning correlate with each other—but only because they both correlate with temperature.

Whenever there's a relationship between two things, we tend to assume that one of them caused the other. But as any good statistician will tell you, correlation does not equal causation.[35] And there are plenty of quite funny statistical findings that illustrate this.[36] For example, during the years of 2000 through 2009:

- The number of people who drowned by falling into a swimming pool correlates with the number of films Nicolas Cage appeared in.

- The per capita cheese consumption correlates with the number of people who died by becoming tangled in their bedsheets.

- The divorce rate in Maine, New England, correlates with the per capita margarine consumption.

How can these things correlate? Well, if you have a big enough pile of data, you can find plenty of variables that just happen to have a statistical correlation.

It's a complete coincidence, but still, it's very tempting to try to come up with an explanation for why Nicolas Cage's movies makes people stumble into pools. It's human nature to force causal links:

- "My friend ignores me because she's mad at me."

- "I failed the test because I suck at math."

- "The team is failing because of the coach."

Explanations like these help us bind facts together, but they're often inaccurate. The world is a complicated place, and we overestimate our ability to understand the connections within it.

Maybe your friend is just having a bad day. Perhaps you failed the test because you've never had a decent math teacher. And the team might be failing because the players aren't putting in the necessary work.

These things are very hard to know for sure, so pay attention to your tendency to presume that one thing caused another. Be skeptical of your assumptions, open to alternative explanations, and willing to change your mind. That way, you'll be less vulnerable to false cause reasoning.

3. False Dilemma

Our tendency to consider only two options even though more exist.

In a 2011 TV commercial,[37] the moving company United Van Lines asked:

"Is United right for your move? Ask yourself, do you want:

- (A) A seamless professional move? or (B) Your possessions set on fire?
- (A) Technology experts to set up your home network? or (B) Raccoons to run amok with your electronics?
- (A) Portable containers to move yourself? or (B) Complete chaos?

If you answered A, call United."

Now, if you're like me, you're not thrilled about the prospect of chaos. You don't want raccoons to fiddle with your electronics. And you certainly don't want to see all your stuff go up in flames.

But does that mean you have to call United the next time you move? The answer, of course, is no. And the reason for that is that their commercial (although admittedly funny) sets up a false dilemma.

This is a fallacy that occurs when only two options are presented even though, in reality, more choices exist. False dilemmas are usually presented as "either this or that" statements, but they can also come in the form of left-out options.

Sometimes they arise unintentionally, but they can also be used as a rhetorical strategy. When used deliberately, the persuader presents an unacceptable option as the only alternative to the one they want you to choose. Here are some examples:

- "Either we increase taxes, or we learn to live with crumbling roads." (There are many other ways to fund infrastructure.)

- "You are either with us or against us." (You can be on neither side.)

- "America: Love it or leave it." (You can enjoy some parts, be critical of others, and still be a citizen.)

- "I thought you were a good person, but you weren't at church today." (Many good people don't attend church.)

- "Either you buy me this book, or you don't think it's important that I learn to read." (You can refuse to buy the book and still value your daughter's education.)

Other varieties include false trilemmas, which is when three options are presented, false quadrilemmas, which is when four options are presented, and so on. Any time certain options are considered the only possibilities when more exist, it's a logical fallacy.

And whether or not it's brought on intentionally, this reasoning flaw can trick you into making choices you wouldn't have made if you had considered all the options available.

So when you're presented with "either this or that" type statements or a limited number of choices, pause and reflect. Ask yourself if the options are truly mutually exclusive and if they are really the only choices available. That will open up your mind to more possibilities and better decisions.

4. Middle Ground

*Our tendency to assume that the middle point
between two extremes must be true.*

In the last chapter we covered the false dilemma fallacy, our tendency to consider only two options even though more exist. The middle ground fallacy is effectively an inverse false dilemma. That is, instead of only considering two options, we only focus on a middle point between them.

Let's say James is convinced that vaccinations causes autism in children. But his friend John, who's a doctor, says that claim has been debunked and proven false. Listening to their discussion, their mutual friend Robert concludes that vaccinations must cause autism sometimes, but not all the time.

While the correct position on a topic often is somewhere between two extremes, that cannot be assumed without considering the evidence.

Sometimes, one of the extreme positions is entirely true, and the other one completely false. When that's the case, a compromise always misses the mark.

Other times, both extreme positions are wrong. And when that's the case, the truth can't be found anywhere in the spectrum between them.

If we don't pay attention to it, the middle ground fallacy can lead to poor reasoning and bad decisions. Let's have a look at some more examples:

- My teacher says it's never okay to skip classes. My friend Michael says it's okay to skip as many classes as you want. Therefore, it's okay to skip class sometimes.

- Jennifer thinks I should follow my doctor's prescription to treat my illness. Linda says I should use holistic medicine. Therefore, I'll take half of my prescriptions and half of the recommendations from holistic medicine.

- William thinks the Philadelphia Eagles will win the game. David thinks the New England Patriots will win. Therefore, I'll place a large bet that the game ends in a tie.

- Some people believe in man-made climate change. Others claim global warming isn't real. Therefore, climate change is real, but people aren't causing it.

- Some people think slavery is wrong. Other people think slavery is right. Therefore, we should allow slavery in some places but not all.

Compromises are often useful, but not always. As the saying goes, half a kitten is not half as cute, it's a bloody mess.

Whenever you're presented with two opposing views, don't automatically assume that the truth has to exist somewhere between them.

Instead, examine the evidence of each claim independently. Ask yourself how likely they are to be true, and if a compromise between them is truly warranted. That will help you make more accurate assumptions and better choices.

5. Slippery Slope

*Our tendency to assume that a minor action
will lead to a major consequence.*

High school student David wants to spend the weekend with his friends, but his mom won't let him. *"You have to study on Saturdays,"* she insists. *"If you don't, your grades will suffer, you won't get into a good university, and you'll end up flipping burgers for the rest of your life!"*

This is a prime example of the slippery slope fallacy: assuming that a relatively small first step will lead to a chain of events that eventually culminates in a significant, usually negative, outcome.

In other words, you assume that if A occurs, then B will follow, and if B occurs, then C will follow. And since C is something you really don't want, you shouldn't allow A to happen.

Some slippery slopes are real, but often they're not, and that's when we've got a slippery slope fallacy on our hands. To analyze this kind of reasoning, we need to examine each link in the chain.

Let's assign some rough probability estimates to every assumption David's mom is making. She's saying that, if he doesn't study on Saturdays:

A: *"Your grades will suffer."* It's possible but not very likely. A lot of students get good grades without studying on weekends. Let's give this a 5 percent probability estimate.

B: *"You won't get into a good university."* That depends on what counts as a good university. David could also be eligible for non-academic scholarships. We'll give this a probability of, say, 10 percent.

C: *"You'll end up flipping burgers for the rest of your life."* This is obviously the weakest link in the chain. It's really nothing but wildly pessimistic speculation. It gets a probability of 0.1 percent.

As you can see, every link in the chain is weak. And the chain as a whole compounds those weaknesses. Here's how the math works out:

.05 x .10 x .001 = There's a 0.0005 percent risk that David's mom's assumption is correct. Not a very slippery slope.

Of course, it's very difficult to predict the likelihood of a complex chain reaction. We can't know if our probability numbers are accurate. But a rough guesstimate can still provide a useful hint about the likelihood of a chain of events.

So when you come across slippery slope assumptions, tease out the links in the chain and ask yourself how likely each of them is to be true. Then keep these two things in mind:

1) The chain is only as strong as its weakest link. If you spot just one weak claim, the entire line of reasoning is also weak.

2) Weaknesses in the links have a compounding effect. The strength of the whole chain is almost always even weaker than its weakest link.

Be skeptical of hypothetical chain reactions, and you'll be much less vulnerable to falling for slippery slope reasoning.

6. Sunk Cost Fallacy

*Our tendency to do things based on how much
time and resources we've invested.*

Imagine that you go to see a movie. You pay for a ticket and take your seat. But about 30 minutes in, you realize that the movie you're watching is terrible. What should you do?

If you're like most people, you'll finish the movie anyway. You've paid for it, after all, and you want to get your money's worth.

But that decision is actually irrational. Why? Because the ticket purchase is a "sunk cost"; it's money already spent that cannot be recovered.

And, as economists will tell you, sunk costs are not taken into account when making rational decisions.

How so? Well, in the movie scenario, you have two choices:

1) Pay the price of the ticket and waste the time it takes to finish it.

2) Pay the price of the ticket and not waste the time it takes to finish it.

Since the second option only involves one loss (money spent), while the first involves two losses (money spent and time wasted), an economist would say that the second option is obviously preferable.

You've already paid for the ticket, so that part of the decision no longer affects the future. Therefore, the current choice should be based solely on whether you want to see the movie at all, regardless of the price, just as if it were free.

Now, of course, that's easier said than done. In reality, we often fall for the "sunk cost fallacy" and routinely let our current actions be affected by the money, time, and effort we've previously invested into something.[38]

This tendency shows up all the time in small everyday decisions like:

- "I'm full, but I might as well keep eating because I've paid for the food."

- "This book is boring, but I've already read 100 pages so I might as well finish it."

- "I haven't used this sweater in years, but it was so expensive that I have to keep it."

And it can also affect big life decisions like:

- "I've invested so much into this business venture that I might as well keep pouring money into it."

- "This career isn't fulfilling to me, but I'll stick to it because I've invested so much time and money into my education."

- "I know my partner is bad for me, but we've been together for so long that it wouldn't make sense to leave."

As you can imagine, the sunk cost fallacy can have a considerable influence on our lives. So, when you make decisions, try to let bygones be bygones. Ignore costs from the past, base your decision solely on the present, and you'll be much better off in the future.

7. Planning Fallacy

Our tendency to underestimate the time and resources needed to complete something.

Do you underestimate the time it will take you to get to work in the morning? Have you ever raced to meet a deadline? Do you struggle to keep your monthly budget?

If your answer to any of these questions is "Yes," then you know what's it's like to fall for the planning fallacy. And you're not alone. Research shows that we all tend to underestimate the time and resources needed to finish things.

A great illustration of this comes from a study in which students were asked to estimate when they would complete their personal academic projects.[39] The results showed that less than half of them finished by the time they were 99 percent sure they would be done. Even when they were asked to make "highly conservative forecasts," predictions the students were pretty much certain they would fulfill, their estimates were still way too optimistic.

And the planning fallacy doesn't just occur in individual tasks. It also affects group projects, which can magnify its consequences dramatically. Consider, for example, the following massive construction overruns:

- The Denver International Airport opened sixteen months later than scheduled with a total cost of $4.8 billion—over $2 billion more than expected.[40]
- The Eurofighter Typhoon, a joint defense project of several European countries, took six years longer and cost €8 billion more than initially planned.[41]

- The Sydney Opera House, originally estimated to be finished in 1963 for $7 million, was completed ten years later for a grand total of $102 million.[42]

I know, crazy, right? Why are we so terrible at estimating the time and resources needed to finish projects? A clue to the underlying problem comes from a study[43] where the researchers found that asking people for their predictions based on realistic "best guess" scenarios, versus hoped-for "best case" scenarios, produced indistinguishable results.

It turns out that when we're asked for a "best guess" scenario, we envision that everything will go exactly as planned. As a result, we end up with a vision that is exactly the same as our "best case." And since reality is full of unforeseen delays, this way of thinking creates a lot of problems, delays, and stress.

A much more useful approach is what researchers call "reference class forecasting": predicting the future by looking at similar past situations and their outcomes. In other words, instead of guessing, you base your plans on available data.

- When planning how much time you need to get ready in the morning, don't imagine what tomorrow morning will be like. Consider how much time you usually need every morning and use that as your estimate.

- When scheduling a project at work, don't guess how long it will take you to complete. Find out how long this kind of project typically takes and plan accordingly.

- When creating your monthly budget, don't just write down what you would ideally like to spend. Look at what you're typically spending each month and start from there.

Planning this way will give you an accurate understanding of the time and resources needed. That will make your plans realistic and useful. As a result, you'll be remarkably productive and efficient.

8. Appeal to Popularity

Our tendency to believe something is true just because it's popular.

Let's begin this chapter with a quick trip down memory lane. When you were a kid, did you ever try to convince your parents to buy you a Pet Rock, Transformer, Furby, or whatever the popular fad toy of your childhood was?

Stating your case, you probably said something like, "Everyone at school has one! And they say it's the best toy ever, so I have to have one, too!" To which, inevitably, your parents responded something like, "If everyone at school jumped off a cliff, would you do it, too?"

With that response, whether or not they knew it, your parents were pointing out a flaw in your reasoning known as "appeal to popularity." This is a fallacy that occurs when something is considered being good, true, or valid solely because it's popular.

The reasoning goes like this: "Everybody is doing X. Therefore, X must be the right thing to do." That kind of thinking is problematic because, as your parents pointed out, the majority isn't always right.

Something can be true, even if everyone believes it's false. And something can be false, even if everyone believes it's true.

When stated in such explicit language, few people think they'd fall for such stupid reasoning. But even among adults it's a remarkably common fallacy. The reason is that our intuition tells us that if an idea is popular, it must have some truth to it.

But ideas don't get popular because they're true. They get popular because they're, well, popular. This phenomenon is called the "bandwagon effect": if an idea gains some attraction, that will, in and of itself, attract more interest.

That interest then generates even more interest and, before you know it, everyone is jumping on the bandwagon and giving their support for the idea. It doesn't matter if the idea is true or not. The bandwagon has its own momentum and will carry its passengers either way.

Now, that doesn't mean that you should completely disregard popular ideas. Sometimes what the majority believes is actually true. For example, if most scientists accept that the universe is about 13.7 billion years old, it's wise to believe them because they can present good evidence for their claim.

But in most cases, it's important to treat appeals to popularity with a healthy dose of skepticism. If you don't, you handicap your judgment and risk making poor decisions. For example:

- *"This book doesn't look all that great, but it has sold a million copies, so I'll buy it."*

- *"It's against the law to lie on your taxes, but everyone does it, so I'll do it, too."*

- *"Everyone at work sleeps just five hours per night, so I'll start cutting back on my sleep."*

In the words of Mark Twain: *"Whenever you find yourself on the side of the majority, it is time to pause and reflect."* Deliberately choose the bandwagons you jump on, and you'll make wiser choices and get better results.

9. Appeal to Authority

*Our tendency to believe something is true just
because it's the opinion of an expert.*

When people present an argument, they sometimes refer to the opinion of some authority as evidence for their claim. This is often a person, but it can also be something like a book, a website, or a constitution.

That kind of reasoning can be problematic, especially if the person insists their claim must be true merely because some authority said so. It is not that an expert says it that makes a claim true. What makes it true is the preponderance of evidence for their theory.

An argument from an authority can never prove that something is true. It can, however, make it more likely to be true. But that's only the case if the authority referred to is actually an expert on the topic at hand.

If the expert is relevant, an appeal to authority is sound. But if the expert is irrelevant, the argument is fallacious. When you come across this kind of reasoning, the trick is to evaluate the relevancy of the expert. Let's look at some examples:

> *"Mozart heavily influenced Beethoven. I know so because I looked it up online."*

This is an appeal to non-authority. It's fallacious because we know nothing about the reliability of the website. The internet as a whole can't be trusted as a reliable authority on anything.

> *"Eating cooked meat causes cancer. I know so because scientists say so."*

This is an appeal to anonymous authorities. It's fallacious since we don't know who these scientists are. If we're unfamiliar with the research, we can't know how reliable it is.

"God doesn't exist. I know so because Stephen Hawking said so."

This is an appeal to unqualified authority. It's fallacious because, while Stephen Hawking was a brilliant physicist, that doesn't automatically make him an authority on whether God exists.

"I need to take my medicine. I know so because my doctor prescribed it."

This is an appeal to legitimate authority. It's not fallacious, because the authority has expertise relevant to the claim. Assuming that the doctor has the right medical training, you can confidently follow the prescription.

Now, there's always a chance that even a highly relevant authority could be wrong, so it's always a good idea to think of facts as provisionally true. Accept information from credible experts as correct, but be willing to change your mind whenever you come across an argument with more trustworthy facts.

Question authority and analyze evidence. That way, you'll be more flexible in your beliefs and less vulnerable to irrelevant expert opinions.

10. The Fallacy Fallacy

*Our tendency to assume that when a fallacy
is made, the claim must be wrong.*

As you learn about the logical fallacies in this book, you'll probably find plenty of examples in your everyday life.

- Maybe someone makes a bad first impression on you, and you conclude he's a rude person. But then you realize that's a hasty generalization. You can't draw that conclusion based on such a small sample size.

- Perhaps a friend tells you that she doesn't feel well because of the fish she ate yesterday. You identify this as a false cause fallacy. She can't know that it's necessarily the fish that caused her to feel bad.

- Someone might recommend a book, telling you that "everyone loves it." And you recognize this as an appeal to popularity. How popular the book is says little about whether you'll enjoy it.

And when you spot a fallacy, it's tempting to think that the claim must be wrong. But that assumption is actually itself a fallacy aptly named the fallacy fallacy. You see, it's entirely possible to reason poorly, use a variety of fallacies, and still arrive at a true conclusion.

- The person you met might actually be rude. You can't know it from just one meeting, but it's fully possible that future encounters will be equally unpleasant.

- Your friend does indeed feel bad because of the fish she had. There are many factors that could have caused it, but the fish might just be the correct one.

- The book someone recommended might just be spectacular. While the claim that "everyone loves it" isn't very useful, it could still turn out to be an excellent read.

The takeaway? A fallacy is never evidence against the claim. It's just evidence for poor reasoning.

Being able to identify logical fallacies is an important skill that can dramatically improve your thinking. But if you concentrate too much on them, you can lose sight of the content within the reasoning. And if you focus too much on calling them out, well, then you'll risk becoming an annoying know-it-all.

So whenever you spot a fallacy, keep this helpful command in mind:

> *"Don't shoot the message. Just because the messenger is stupid, doesn't mean the message is."*[44]

PART 4: MENTAL MODELS

Point of view is worth 80 IQ points.

—Alan Kay

The Thinking Tools of the Mind

"Why did the chicken cross the road?"

According to biologist Robert Sapolsky, the answer to that question will depend on the expert you ask.[45] For example:

- A biologist might say: "The chicken crossed the road because it saw a potential mate on the other side."

- A kinesiologist might say: "The chicken crossed the road because the muscles in its legs contracted and pulled its leg bones forward."

- A neuroscientist might say: "The chicken crossed the road because the neurons in its brain fired and triggered it to move."

Interestingly, all of these experts are correct. But at the same time, none of them are seeing the entire picture. And that's because all of them are looking at the question through the lens of their unique expertise.

Mental Models

A mental model is a representation of how something works. It's a concept, framework, or worldview stored in your mind that you use to interpret, simplify, and understand the world. For example:

- Second-Level Thinking is a mental model that helps you identify subsequent consequences before they happen.

- Incentives is a mental model that helps you understand what motivates people.

- Entropy is a mental model that helps you understand how everything in life moves from order to disorder.

Mental models guide your perceptions, thoughts, and actions. They are the thinking tools your mind uses to explain reality, solve problems, and make decisions.

The Limitations of Expertise

The quality of your decisions depends on the mental models in your mind. If you have a lot of mental models—a big toolbox—you're better equipped to perceive reality accurately and find solutions to problems.

Most of us, however, don't have a big toolbox to pick and choose from. Instead, we default back to just a few tools again and again. Usually, these are mental models related to our discipline and expertise.

A biologist will tend to think in terms of evolution. A kinesiologist will tend to think in terms of mechanisms of movement. And a neuroscientist will tend to think in terms of the nervous system and the brain.

The more you master a particular mental model, the more you'll start applying it everywhere. You'll cram reality into your model of it. And so what looks like expertise can actually become a limitation.

As the proverb goes: "If all you have is a hammer, everything looks like a nail."

Expanding Your Toolbox

If your set of mental models is limited, so is your ability to find solutions. To make wise choices, you have to collect a wide range of mental models. In other words, you have to have a well-equipped decision-making toolbox.

The good news? Acquiring new thinking tools is straightforward. Once you learn a mental model, you can't unlearn it. And from that point forward, you can use it anytime you want to shift your perspective and find new solutions.

What's more, you don't have to master every idea from every discipline to become a great thinker. If you can just get a firm grasp of a few fundamental models, you'll develop a remarkably accurate and useful picture of reality.

In the chapters ahead, we'll cover the most widely applicable mental models for decision-making. And we'll begin with a very useful idea for understanding how the mind works.

1. System 1 and System 2

The two modes of thought.

Imagine that I ask you, "What's 2 + 2?"

You can't help but think of the answer. The number "4" instantly pops into your head. If you've learned basic math, it's impossible not to immediately think of the answer. This is the result of what scientists call reflexive brain.

Now, imagine that I instead ask you, "What's 39 multiplied by 26?"

Most likely, your brain goes blank. It doesn't have an instant answer. Unless you're a math wizard, you have to go through the tedious process of calculating it. You have to use what is known as your reflective brain.

In his book *Thinking Fast and Slow*, Daniel Kahneman termed these two modes of thought as System 1 (reflexive) and System 2 (reflective):[46]

> *"System 1 operates automatically and quickly, with little or no effort and no sense of voluntary control. System 2 allocates attention to the effortful mental activities that demand it, including complex computations."*

In other words, System 1 is intuitive, and System 2 is deliberate. These two modes of thought complement each other, and they're both active whenever we're awake.

System 1 is the first layer of thinking that our brains delegate problems to. System 2 only comes into the picture when System 1 doesn't have an answer.

That arrangement usually works pretty well because System 1 is generally good at what it does. It's not perfect, however, and there are many situations where decisions should ideally be delegated to System 2, but System 1 makes them anyway.

As an example, consider the simple math problem below. Don't try to solve it—just observe the intuitive answer that comes to mind:

The total cost of a baseball bat and ball is $1.10. The cost of the bat is $1.00 more than the ball. How much does the ball cost?

System 1 will tell you that the ball costs 10 cents, which is the wrong answer. If you do the math using System 2, you'll realize that the right answer is 5 cents (and $1.05 for the bat).

This example illustrates the problem with System 1. While fast and effortless, it's also prone to mistakes. In fact, the sloppiness of System 1 is what creates the cognitive biases and logical fallacies we covered previously in the book.

But despite its flaws, you shouldn't try to turn off System 1 and operate solely in System 2. According to Kahneman, that wouldn't be possible nor desirable:[47]

> *"Constantly questioning our own thinking would be impossibly tedious, and System 2 is much too slow and inefficient to serve as a substitute for System 1 in making routine decisions. The best we can do is a compromise: learn to recognize situations in which mistakes are likely and try harder to avoid significant mistakes when the stakes are high."*

When you're making mundane and inconsequential decisions, let System 1 run. It's okay that it's wrong now and again because it saves valuable mental energy and reduces decision fatigue.

But when you're about to make an important decision, switch to System 2. Deliberately slow down, take your time, and use the mental models in the chapters ahead to reach the best decision possible.

2. The Map Is Not the Territory

An abstraction derived from something is not the thing itself.

In 1931, mathematician Alfred Korzybski presented a paper in which he introduced the idea that the map is not the territory.[48] A map always comes with certain inherent problems. Here are some of its limitations:

- A map can be wrong without you realizing it.
- A map is by definition a reduction of the territory, which means it leaves out certain important information.
- A map needs interpretation, which is a process that often leads to mistakes.
- A map can be outdated and represent something that has changed or no longer exists.

The distinction between map and territory is a useful metaphor of the differences between impression and reality. What you think something is like differs from what it's really like.

Imagine, for example, that you're checking out the social media profile of an acquaintance. Browsing through her countless updates of happy pictures, you conclude that she has to be a happy person. But the map is not the territory. The life she's portraying on social media says little about what her life is really like.

And there are many other examples of where we confuse the map with the territory. A commercial is not the product. An online dating profile is not the person. A documentary is not the complete picture. A resume is not the applicant. A test score is not your intelligence.

On a deeper level, your perceptions of reality can also be considered maps. Your brain takes what you perceive through your senses and creates maps of reality written in neural patterns. And that kind of map is just as problematic as any other.

Why? Well, firstly, our senses are neurologically limited and only operate within a certain bandwidth. Our brains are not equipped to perceive the full range of reality. Which is why, for example, we can't hear the ultrasonic sounds of a bat.

Secondly, as we've seen in previous chapters, our minds are heavily influenced by cognitive biases that distort our thinking and logical fallacies that derail our reasoning. Which is why, for example, we unduly favor information that confirms our existing beliefs.

So as we create our inner representations of the external world, we do so using incomplete and distorted information. As a result, we often end up with beliefs that don't match up with reality.

A map is never the same as the territory, and most of us struggle to make that distinction. In the words of author Shane Parrish:

> *"For many people, the model creates its own reality. It is as if the spreadsheet comes to life. We forget that reality is a lot messier. The map isn't the territory. The theory isn't what it describes, it's simply a way we choose to interpret a certain set of information. Maps can also be wrong, but even if they are essentially correct, they are an abstraction, and abstraction means that information is lost to save space."*[49]

Be skeptical of maps. Remember their limitations. And always be willing to switch them out whenever you find a better one. That way, you'll be less rigid in your thinking and more accurate in your judgments. And that's a great foundation for making intelligent decisions.

3. The 80/20 Principle

80 percent of the effects come from 20 percent of the causes.

In the late 1800s, Italian economist Vilfredo Pareto was tending his garden when he made a small discovery that would have huge implications.

He noticed that a minority of the pea pods in his garden produced a majority of the peas. And that got him thinking about economic output on a larger scale. Could this unequal distribution be taking place in other areas as well?

At the time, Pareto was studying the wealth of different nations. As he started analyzing the distribution of wealth in his home country, he indeed found that about 80 percent of the land in Italy was owned by just 20 percent of the population. Expanding his work into other countries, Pareto found that a similar distribution applied in those places, too.[50]

Similar to the pea pods in his garden, the majority of resources were controlled by a minority of the group. And as he continued his research in various societies, industries, and even companies, this trend turned out to be remarkably consistent. The numbers were never quite the same, but the approximate 4-to-1 ratio kept showing up.

Over time, this idea—that a minority of things account for the majority of results—became known as the Pareto Principle or, as it's commonly referred to these days, the 80/20 principle.[51]

Since Pareto's discovery, the 80/20 principle has been most popular in business settings. Companies have often found that, for example:

- 20 percent of their customers brought in 80 percent of their revenue.

- 20 percent of their sales reps closed 80 percent of their sales.

- 20 percent of their costs made up 80 percent of their total expenses.

And that's valuable information that can help increase efficiency and profits for companies. But the 80/20 principle is just as useful outside of business. You can ask yourself, for instance:

- Which 20 percent of your relationships create 80 percent of your happiness?

- What 20 percent of your daily habits account for 80 percent of your well-being?

- What 20 percent of your stuff do you use 80 percent of the time?

By answering questions like these, you can increase the efficiencies in your life. You'll know who to spend your time with, what daily habits to focus on, and what clothes to keep in your closet.

And those are just a few examples, of course. The 80/20 principle is very useful anytime you want to figure out the most impactful causes and efficient actions.

In fact, it's a great way to consume this book. As you keep reading, think about which 20 percent of the chapters will provide 80 percent of usefulness to you. Then focus on learning those ideas first.

Get into the habit of thinking 80/20, and you'll spend a lot more time on what's truly essential.

4. The Circle of Competence

The subject area that matches a person's skills or expertise.

In his 1996 shareholder letter,[52] legendary investor Warren Buffett wrote:

> *"What an investor needs is the ability to correctly evaluate selected businesses. Note that word "selected": You don't have to be an expert on every company, or even many. You only have to be able to evaluate companies within your circle of competence. The size of that circle is not very important; knowing its boundaries, however, is vital."*

Everyone builds up knowledge on certain areas throughout their lives. Some areas are widely understood, while others require more specific expertise.

For example, most of us have a basic understanding of the economics of a restaurant. You buy or rent a place, furnish it, and hire employees to cook, serve, and clean.

From there, it's all about setting the right prices and generating enough traffic to make a profit on what you serve after your expenses have been paid.

The menu, atmosphere, and pricing will vary, but all restaurants follow the same economic formula. That basic knowledge, combined with some understanding of accounting and a little bit of study, is enough to allow you to evaluate and invest in restaurants. It's not too complicated.

However, most of us don't have the same understanding of how a biotech drug company works. And, according to Buffett, that's perfectly fine. To be a successful investor, you don't have to understand every business you come across. But you have to understand what you know—your circle of competence—and stick to those areas.

Buffett's business partner Charlie Munger applies this idea to life in general:[53]

> *"You have to figure out what your own aptitudes are. If you play games where other people have the aptitudes and you don't, you're going to lose. And that's as close to certain as any prediction that you can make. You have to figure out where you've got an edge. And you've got to play within your own circle of competence."*

To give you a concrete example, I'll share my circle of competence. It contains three major areas:

1) Writing. This is the number one keystone habit of my business. So before I do anything else each day, I write for at least two hours.

2) Learning. To be a good writer, I need a lot of good ideas to write about. So I spend time every day educating myself on things my readers want to learn about.

3) Marketing. I want to reach and serve as many people as possible. To do that, I spend a lot of time learning about stuff like online marketing, persuasion, consumer psychology, and so on.

Each workday that I learn something, write something, and promote what I wrote, I consider a day well spent. Conversely, each workday I stray outside of these three areas, I generally see as a day poorly spent.

That's the power of a well-defined circle of competence. It makes you a lot less vulnerable to the Dunning-Kruger effect. You'll be acutely aware of what you know and what you don't know. And that helps you spend your time, energy, and resources much more efficiently.

What's your circle of competence? Do you know its boundaries? And are you operating inside of it?

5. Opportunity Cost

The benefits missed when choosing one option over another.

Imagine a stove with four burners on it that each represents a major area of your life:

- The first burner is your family.
- The second burner is your friends.
- The third burner is your health.
- The fourth burner is your work.

The Four Burners Theory says, "In order to be successful, you have to cut off one of your burners. And in order to be really successful, you have to cut off two."[54]

If you want a successful career and a happy marriage, then you won't have as much time for working out and seeing your friends. If you want to be healthy and succeed as a parent, then you won't have as much time to put into your career.

Of course, you can choose to spend your time equally among all four burners, but then you'll never achieve your full potential in any of the areas.

It's quite a predicament, and there's no perfect solution for it. But the Four Burners Theory is still useful because it highlights an important fact of life that we tend to overlook:

Making decisions requires trading off one goal against another.[55]

We continuously face decisions between the benefits and costs of one option and the benefits and costs of another option. The problem is that the benefits are usually much more readily apparent than the costs.

And that's why it's important to understand the concept economists call opportunity cost: "the loss of potential gain from other alternatives when one alternative is chosen."

You can think of it this way: Every time you say yes to something, you're also saying no to something else. The thing you say no to would have given you certain benefits. And now that you're not getting them, they are your opportunity costs.

Imagine, for example, that you're browsing Amazon looking for a book to read. When you find an interesting title, all the possible benefits are readily available on the book page. But what is less obvious is the opportunity cost of the book. That is, the benefits from the other books you could read instead.

Considering opportunity costs in your decisions is important because it helps you to assess different courses of action more accurately. Before I knew about it, I jumped on a lot of exciting business opportunities that came my way because I focused solely on the benefits.

But I've since learned that each of these endeavors comes with a steep opportunity cost. Every time I say yes to some appealing new opportunity, I also say no to researching, writing, and marketing my books. Sure, I might gain some nice short-term benefits, but they're rarely worth straying outside my circle of competence and losing momentum in my author career.

How about you? In what areas of your life do you need to start considering the opportunity costs? And what changes do you need to make to get the greatest return on your limited time, energy, and money?

6. The Eisenhower Matrix

Prioritizing what's important over what's urgent.

Dwight D. Eisenhower lived a remarkably productive life.

From 1953 to 1961, he served two terms as President of the United States. During that time, he initiated several programs that directly led to, among many other things, the development of the Interstate Highway System, the launch of the internet, and the establishment of NASA.

Before his time in office, he was a five-star general in the United States Army. Serving as Supreme Allied Commander in Europe during the Second World War, he was responsible for planning and executing invasions of Germany, France, and North Africa.

At other points during his career, Eisenhower also served as president of Columbia University as well as the first ever Supreme Commander of NATO. And, as if all that wasn't enough, he also somehow made time for hobbies like golfing, cooking, and oil painting.

Considering his incredible ability to get things done, it's no surprise that his time management methods are still being taught to this day. His most famous productivity strategy is called the Eisenhower Matrix,[56] and it's a very useful model for prioritizing your tasks. To use it, you sort your tasks into four categories depending on their importance and urgency:

1) Important and urgent–Tasks you will do immediately.

2) Important but not urgent–Tasks you will schedule for later.

3) Not important but urgent–Tasks you will delegate.

4) Not important nor urgent–Tasks you will eliminate.

The key here is to distinguish between important and urgent tasks. So what's the difference? *Important* tasks are things that contribute to your long-term goals. *Urgent* tasks are things that require immediate attention. To give you an example of what an Eisenhower Matrix might look like, here's mine for today:

	URGENT	NOT URGENT
IMPORTANT	**IMPORTANT AND URGENT** • WRITING THE CHAPTER ON THE EISENHOWER MATRIX.	**IMPORTANT, BUT NOT URGENT** • RESEARCHING UPCOMING CHAPTERS. • REVIEWING MY BOOK MARKETING CAMPAIGN. • GOING TO THE GYM.
NOT IMPORTANT	**NOT IMPORTANT, BUT URGENT** • ANSWERING THE PHONE. • REPLYING TO MOST E-MAILS. • RESPONDING TO FACEBOOK MESSAGES.	**NOT IMPORTANT OR URGENT** • WATCHING TELEVISION. • CHECKING SOCIAL MEDIA. • BROWSING THE INTERNET.

The great thing about this matrix is how widely applicable it is. You can use it as you plan out your year, day, or next hour. No matter the time frame, it helps you filter out the noise so you can focus your limited time, energy, and attention where it truly matters.

Connecting it to the mental models we've covered so far, the

Eisenhower Matrix helps you uncover your 80/20 tasks, stay within your circle of competence, and reduce the opportunity costs that come with doing what's urgent instead of important.

So as you decide what to do next, ask yourself, "Is this important or urgent?" If it's truly important, go ahead and do it now or schedule it for later. But if it's just urgent, try to delegate or delete it altogether.

That way, you'll make more efficient choices, minimize unnecessary stress, and increase your productivity.

7. First Principles Thinking

*Breaking down problems into their basic
parts and reassembling them.*

In 2002, technology entrepreneur Elon Musk began his mission to send the first rocket to Mars. And right away, he ran into a major problem.

After visiting several aerospace manufacturers around the world, he found that the cost of a rocket was enormous—as much as $65 million.

But he didn't let that faze him. Instead, he started to rethink his approach. In an interview with *Wired*,[57] he said:

> *I tend to approach things from a physics framework. And physics teaches you to reason from first principles rather than by analogy. So I said, OK, let's look at the first principles. What is a rocket made of? Aerospace-grade aluminum alloys, plus some titanium, copper, and carbon fiber. And then I asked, what is the value of those materials on the commodity market? It turned out that the materials cost of a rocket was around 2 percent of the typical price.*

Instead of getting a ready-made rocket, Musk decided to create his own company, buy the cheap raw materials, and build it himself. And within just a few years, his company SpaceX had cut the cost of launching a rocket by almost ten times while still making a profit.

First principles thinking means breaking down complicated problems into basic elements and then reassembling them from the ground up. It's one of the most powerful ways to learn how to think for yourself, unlock your creativity, and come up with innovative ideas.

Few of us approach our problems that way. Instead, we reason by analogy, relying on prior assumptions, beliefs, and widely held "best practices" to build knowledge and solve problems. And while that requires less mental energy, it also gets us stuck in existing conventions.

How can you use first principles thinking in your life? Here is Elon Musk's three-step process:[58]

Step 1: Identify and define your current assumptions.

Step 2: Break down the problem into its fundamental principles.

Step 3: Create new solutions from scratch.

Since most of us aren't building space rockets anytime soon, let's apply this process to a more relatable problem. Let's say, for example, that you're struggling to find the time to work out. To solve that problem, your steps might look something like this:

1) Working out requires me to go to the gym and, with my busy schedule, there's just no time for that.

2) To increase my fitness, all I really have to do is work out at a level that my body isn't used to.

3) I could try a quick high-intensity interval training routine like the seven-minute workout.

Working out doesn't require a lot of time at the gym. But if you rely on reasoning by analogy, it's easy to forget about that.

And that's why first principles thinking is so useful. It helps you shake off prior assumptions so you can find more innovative solutions.

So, whenever you face a complicated problem, try breaking it down and reassembling it. That way, you'll step outside conventional wisdom and see what's truly possible.

8. Second-Level Thinking

Identifying subsequent consequences before they happen.

In his book *The Most Important Thing*, investor Howard Marks explains the difference between first- and second-level thinking:[59]

> *First-level thinking is simplistic and superficial, and just about everyone can do it (a bad sign for anything involving an attempt at superiority). All the first-level thinker needs is an opinion about the future, as in "The outlook for the company is favorable, meaning the stock will go up." Second-level thinking is deep, complex and convoluted.*

First-level thinkers look for answers that are quick and easy. Second-level thinkers look for solutions at the second, third, and nth order.

The ability to move past first-level thinking is crucial to avoid poor decisions and costly mistakes. That's because second-level thinking is how you identify the consequences of a decision before they happen.

Consider, for example, the introduction of the cane toad in Australia. In 1935, about 3,000 of these warty amphibians were released in the sugarcane plantations in north Queensland with the hope that they would hunt and kill cane-destroying beetles in the area.

Unfortunately, the cane toads turned out to be bad beetle hunters, partly because the cane fields provide inadequate shelter during the day, and partly because the beetles live at the tops of sugar canes, and the toads are bad climbers.

They have, however, been remarkably successful at reproducing and spreading themselves. Today, there are millions, if not billions, of cane toads in Australia. Their still-expanding range covers thousands of square miles in the northeastern part of the country.

And while they haven't been effective in reducing beetles, they've had marked effects in other parts of Australia's ecology. Examples include the depletion of native species, the poisoning of pets and humans, depletion of native fauna, and reduced prey populations for native insectivores, such as skinks.

Because of all that, cane toads are now considered pests themselves, and government eradication efforts include asking residents to help collect and dispose of them.[60]

Whoops. First-level thinking: These toads will kill the pests we hate. Second-level thinking: These toads have few natural predators here, they breed easily, and they'll have abundant food. They will become the pests.

The takeaway? When you're facing a complex problem or difficult decision, think deeply about the knock-on effects of each solution or option. Howard Marks outlines his process for second-level thinking as a series of questions like:[61]

- *What is the range of likely future outcomes?*
- *Which outcome do I think will occur?*
- *What's the probability I'm right?*
- *What does the consensus think?*
- *How does my expectation differ from the consensus?*

By digging deeper than the first level, and carefully evaluating what you find at the levels below, you can spot negative consequences before they arise. And that will help you make better decisions and avoid serious mistakes.

9. Inversion

Thinking backward instead of forward.

During his career, the German mathematician Carl Jacobi made important contributions to several scientific fields. In his work, he often solved difficult problems by following his maxim "man muss immer umkehren," which loosely translates into "invert, always invert."[62]

Jacobi believed that one of the best ways to clarify your thinking is to restate problems in their inverse form. He would write down the opposite of the math problems he was trying to solve and found that the solutions often came more easily to him.

While Jacobi mainly applied inversion to mathematics, it's an equally powerful approach in other areas. No matter what problems you're trying to solve, it can help you uncover errors and roadblocks that aren't readily apparent.

The way to use inversion is to think about things backward instead of forward. Rather than asking how to do something, you ask how *not* to do it. Let's have a look at some examples of what those questions might look like.

Career

- What kind of work feels uninteresting and meaningless to me?
- What is outside my circle of competence?
- What industries have low or decreasing demand?

Business

- What would alienate our core customer?

- How can we become less innovative?
- How can we create a negative company culture?

Productivity

- How can I waste more time on distractions?
- How can I shatter my focus every day?
- How can I reduce the energy I bring to my work?

Health

- How can I decrease the quality and quantity of my sleep?
- What foods can I eat more of to lower my energy and increase the risk of disease?
- How can I make sure I move less every day?

Relationships

- How can I be a bad friend?
- How can I be a terrible leader?
- How can I ruin my marriage?

If you're like most people, you rarely ask yourself questions like these. For most of us, inversion is highly counterintuitive. Thinking backward is not something that comes naturally to us.

But it's very much worth practicing because it helps improve your understanding of problems. It forces you to step out of your status quo bias, consider different perspectives, and come up with new options.

Inverting problems won't always solve them, but it will help you avoid trouble. When you know what you don't want, you can take steps to make sure those things don't happen. And that will move you closer to the solution.

So, whenever the best path forward isn't clear, flip the problem on its head. Instead of trying to find the right path to take, make sure you know which ones to avoid.

Keep in mind: "Invert, always invert."

Spend less time trying to be smart and more time trying to avoid being stupid. Avoiding mistakes is generally much easier than seeking excellence—and it's usually a much better way to solve your problems.

10. Bayesian Thinking

Estimating probabilities using prior knowledge.

Thomas Bayes was an eighteenth-century English statistician, philosopher, and minister. His most famous work was "An Essay towards Solving a Problem in the Doctrine of Chances," which he never published himself. Instead, it was introduced to the Royal Society two years after his death by his friend Richard Price.

The essay contained the seeds of what today is called Bayes Theorem, which "describes the probability of an event, based on prior knowledge of conditions that might be related to the event."[63]

If you're not into math, don't worry. You don't have to understand exactly how probability calculations work to benefit from Bayesian thinking. You just have to grasp the intuitions behind the math, which is easy to do. Consider, for example, the following news headline: **Violent Crime Doubles**

If you read that in your local newspaper, you might get worried that your chances of being assaulted have increased dramatically. But is that really true? To find out, we'll use Bayesian thinking to put this new piece of information into the context of your prior knowledge.

Let's say that violent crime in your city has been declining steadily for decades. You know that the risk of being assaulted last year was 1 in 10,000. Since then, according to the news article, violent crime has doubled. That means the risk of assault is now 2 in 10,000. In other words, the risk of getting assaulted is no longer 0.01 percent, but 0.02 percent.

So the headline actually shouldn't make you too worried. Sure, the probability of getting assaulted has increased. It has indeed doubled. But it's still very unlikely to happen. And that's difficult to discern unless you factor in prior information about the situation.

This example illustrates the big idea behind Bayes Theorem: that we should continuously update our probability estimates about things as we come across new information. And that's very different from how we typically approach the world. Usually, we tend to either completely dismiss new evidence or embrace it as though nothing else matters.

As an example of that, let's say that you consider yourself a good driver. But then, one day, you get into a car accident. In that situation, most people will either protect their belief ("It was the other guy's fault") or replace it altogether ("I guess I'm a terrible driver").

By instead using Bayesian thinking, you look at the situation in the context of your prior experience. Sure, the car accident is evidence against your theory that you're a good driver. But that doesn't mean you stubbornly have to protect or immediately replace that belief. It just means you should be a little less confident that it's accurate.

Instead of being 100 percent or 0 percent sure that your theory is correct, you assign it a more reasonable probability. If you've been driving for ten years with no prior accidents, perhaps you can now be 90 percent sure that you're a good driver. With that estimate in mind, you don't have to avoid driving, but you might want to be a little more cautious than you were previously.

Reasoning this way makes you much more aware that your beliefs are grey scale rather than black and white. It allows you to continually update the level of confidence in your own theories about the world. And that helps you make more accurate predictions, improve your decisions, and get better outcomes.

11. Multiplying by Zero

Anything times zero is always zero.

In 1986, college basketball prodigy Leonard "Len" Bias was selected as the second overall pick in the NBA Draft by the Boston Celtics. It seemed like he had everything needed to become one of the best basketball players in the world.

- He was 6 ft 9 in (2.06 m), incredibly skillful, and amazingly athletic.

- He lived in Maryland, a place that reveres basketball, and had great support from his parents.

- He had a proven track record, getting two Atlantic Coast Conference Player of the Year awards and named into two All-American teams.

There was just one problem. Bias had developed a cocaine habit, and two days after they picked him in the NBA draft, he passed away from an overdose.

Today, many sportswriters consider Bias to be the greatest basketball player who never played professionally.[64] And what his tragic destiny illustrates is a simple rule we've all learned in math class: anything times zero is always zero. It doesn't matter what the other numbers are—if you multiply them by zero, the answer will inevitably also be zero.

$$1 \times 0 = 0$$

$$128 \times 16 \times 0 = 0$$

$$1{,}577{,}404 \times 99{,}503 \times 6.76 \times 0 = 0$$

Len Bias had incredibly high "numbers" in terms of talent, support, and track record. But in the end, none of that mattered because as soon as he added the "zero" of his cocaine addiction to the equation, the end result was zero.

That's the profound insight behind this simple mathematical fact: all of your talent and hard work can be eradicated entirely by just one weak link in the chain. Let's have a look at some examples.

- You can have everything working for you in your career—a great education, an excellent resume, and an impressive background—but none of that matters if you can't deal with other people.

- Your company might seem impressive—big-name investors, large offices, fancy systems, tons of employees, and a great product or service—but it'll still struggle to be profitable if your customer service is terrible.

- You can get every productivity tool on the market—fancy apps for project management, communication, time-tracking, note-making, and email management—but that won't help you if you're constantly distracted by email and social media.

- You can have plenty of healthy habits—get regular exercise, eat healthy, and meditate every morning—but if you're not sleeping sufficiently, you'll still have an increased risk of cancer, heart attack, and Alzheimer's disease.

- You can be an excellent partner in pretty much every aspect—a great listener, accepting, supportive, and fun to be with—but your relationship can still fall apart if you spend too much time at work.

No matter what you want to accomplish, examine the most critical factors in getting there. Tease out and strengthen the weakest part of the chain. That way, you'll ensure all your hard work isn't for nothing.

12. Occam's Razor

The simplest solution tends to be the right one.

William of Occam was a fourteenth-century English friar, philosopher, and theologian. He's considered one of the prominent figures of medieval thought and was involved in many major intellectual and political controversies during his time.

William is most commonly known for the methodological principle called Occam's razor.[65] He did not coin the term himself, but his way of reasoning inspired other thinkers to develop it.

Occam's razor is basically a rule of thumb for problem-solving which states, "Among competing hypotheses, the one with the fewest assumptions should be selected." Another way of putting it is that the simplest solution is probably correct.

Using Occam's razor, you "cut away" what's excessively complex so you can focus on what works. This approach is used in a wide range of situations to improve judgment and support better decisions. To understand how, let's have a look at a few examples.

Science

Many great scientists have used Occam's razor in their work. Albert Einstein is one of them. His version of the same principle was "Everything should be made as simple as possible, but not simpler." This preference for simplicity shows in his famous equation $E=MC^2$. Rather than settling for a complex, lengthy equation, Einstein boiled it down to its bare minimum.

Medicine

Medical interns are often instructed: "When you hear hoofbeats, think of horses, not zebras." The underlying idea is to always consider obvious explanations for symptoms before turning to more unlikely diagnoses. This version of Occam's razor helps physicians reduce the risk of overtreating patients or causing dangerous interactions between different treatments.

Crime

By using a combination of statistical knowledge and experience, Occam's razor can be used in solving crimes. For example, women are statistically more likely to be killed by a male partner than anyone else. So, if a woman is found in her locked home murdered, the first person to look for is any male partners. By focusing on the most likely perpetrators first, the police can solve crime more efficiently.

As a mental model, Occam's razor works best for making initial conclusions with limited information. To use it, you compare the complexity of different options and favor the simplest one.

Imagine, for example, that you come home one day and find that your living room window is open. This surprises you, as you're usually very diligent in closing it. There are two possible explanations for this:

1) You had a lot on your mind when you left and forgot to close it.

2) Someone has broken into your home while you were away.

The first explanation only requires a little mindlessness on your part. The second explanation, however, means someone had to open your window from the outside, disarm your alarm, avoid detection by neighbors, clean up behind them, and leave just as quietly as they came. Therefore, in the absence of any evidence to the contrary, the first explanation is the simplest and the most likely to be correct.

Occam's razor obviously isn't perfect. There are exceptions to every rule, and you should never follow them blindly. But, in general, favoring the simple over the complex will improve your judgment and help you solve problems faster and better.

13. Hanlon's Razor

*Never attribute to malice that which can be
adequately explained by neglect.*

Do you ever feel like the world is against you? If so, you are not alone. We all tend to assume that when things go wrong, it's because the people in our lives are conspiring against us.

Your colleague didn't tell you about an important meeting? He must be trying to make you look bad and beat you to the promotion. Your friends met up without inviting you? They must be going behind your back because they don't like you anymore. Your kids put finger paint all over your kitchen wall? They must be trying to drive you insane.

But in reality, these explanations aren't likely to be true. It's much more probable that your colleague simply forgot to tell you, that your friends assumed you were busy, and that your kids have yet to learn the difference between a kitchen wall and a canvas. And that's why Hanlon's razor is such a handy tool.

Hanlon's razor is an adage, coined by Robert J. Hanlon, which is best summarized as "Never attribute to malice that which can be adequately explained by neglect." It's essentially a special case of Occam's razor which, as we covered in the last chapter, states, "Among competing hypotheses, the one with the fewest assumptions should be selected."

In a situation where something can be explained either by malice or neglect, the latter is more likely. Malice is a big assumption, but negligence is not. People rarely have genuinely bad intentions, but they make mistakes all the time. And by applying Hanlon's razor in our interactions with others, we can negate the effects of many of our cognitive biases. For example:

The Fundamental Attribution Error

We tend to blame the mistakes of others on their personality, and our own mistakes on the circumstances. If someone else is driving too fast, it's because they're an inconsiderate idiot. But if we're the one who's speeding, it's because the situation warrants it. Hanlon's razor helps us assign situational reasons to everyone's mistakes—not just our own.

The Availability Bias

We often misjudge the frequency of recent events, especially if they're vivid and memorable. Many of us keep a mental scorecard of other people's mistakes. When a new mistake is made, it's magnified by errors in the past, and we start to imagine malicious intent. Hanlon's razor helps us see each mistake as an isolated occurrence.

The Confirmation Bias

We have a tendency to seek out information that confirms our preexisting beliefs. If we expect malicious intent, we are likely to attribute it whenever possible. Hanlon's razor helps us stop looking for confirming evidence so we can accurately identify honest mistakes.

So, whenever you feel mistreated, keep in mind: "Never attribute to malice that which can be adequately explained by neglect." It will make you less judgmental and more empathetic. You'll be able to give other people the benefit of the doubt. And that will make for better relationships and a lot less stress.

Of course, there are people out there who do have malicious intent, and that needs to be taken into account. You don't want to be blind to behavior that is intended to be harmful. But, as a rule of thumb, assuming neglect before malice will make you more accurate in your judgments—and a better fellow human.

14. Incentives

Things that motivate someone to do something.

At the time of French colonial rule of Hanoi, Vietnam, the government was worried about the number of rats in the city, so they created a bounty program that paid a reward for every rat killed. The arrangement was simple: provide a severed rat tail, and you'll get a bounty.

It seemed like a decent enough incentive system. But soon, colonial officials noticed something peculiar—rats without tails started to show up in Hanoi.

In a striking demonstration of the importance of second-level thinking, rat hunters would capture rats, sever their tails, and set them free. That way, the rats could procreate and increase the revenue of the rat hunters.

The government had requested rat tails, and they got exactly what they asked for. But in the process, they motivated the wrong behavior and failed miserably in achieving their intended goal. And that makes the Great Hanoi Rat Hunt[66] a great example of an incentive system gone awry.

The takeaway here is that incentives matter a lot. They lie at the root of many situations we face, and yet we often fail to account for them. To get a deeper and more structured understanding of incentives, we'll turn to behavioral psychology.

If we like the consequences of an action we've taken, we're more likely to do it again. And if we don't like the consequences of an action we've taken, we're less likely to do it again.

That's the basic assumption behind what psychologists call operant conditioning: "a learning process through which the strength of a behavior is modified by reinforcement or punishment."[67]

If you want to change behavior, there are two primary tools at your disposal, reinforcement, which strengthens the behavior, and punishment, which weakens the behavior.

Research shows that consistency and timing are crucial for reinforcement. The best way to learn a new behavior is through continuous reinforcement, in which the behavior is reinforced every time it occurs. Meanwhile, the best way to maintain an already established behavior is through intermittent reinforcement, in which the behavior is reinforced only some of the time.

Let's say that you want to teach your dog to sit. Initially, the best strategy is to reward every successful attempt. Later, when your dog knows how to sit, it's better to reward it sometimes.

Punishment has several issues that generally make it less effective than reinforcement. Firstly, behavior tends to return when the punishment is removed. Secondly, punishment tends to lead to increased fear, stress, and aggression. And thirdly, punishment is a poor guide because it doesn't tell you what to do—only what not to do.

So when you feel tempted to punish a behavior, remember that it's usually more effective to manipulate the reinforcers involved instead.

If you want to stop your dog from begging for food, it's a good strategy to ignore every attempt (no matter how cute) and instead reward it when it doesn't beg.

You generally get the behavior you reward, so whenever you want to change behavior, carefully consider the reinforcers in play. Create an effective incentive system, and the desired behavior will follow.

15. Nudging

*Subtle cues or context changes that gently
push you toward a certain decision.*

In their book, *Nudge*, Richard H. Thaler and Cass R. Sunstein explain that small and seemingly insignificant details in the environment can have a big impact on people's choices and behaviors:

"A wonderful example of this principle comes from, of all places, the men's rooms at Schiphol Airport in Amsterdam. There the authorities have etched the image of a black housefly into each urinal. It seems that men usually do not pay much attention to where they aim, which can create a bit of a mess, but if they see a target, attention and therefore accuracy is much increased."[68]

The result? According to economist Aad Kieboom, who came up with the urinal fly idea, these simple etchings reduce spillage by 80 percent!

That's a remarkable result and a great illustration of the power of "nudging:" small, simple, and inexpensive changes to the environment that increase the likelihood that people will make certain choices or behave in particular ways. Researchers have found several effective nudging techniques, including:

- Default option—People are more likely to choose whatever is presented as the default option. For example, one study found that more consumers chose renewable energy for electricity when it was offered as the default choice.[69]

- Social proof—People tend to look to the behavior of other people to help guide their own. Studies have found that leveraging that tendency can be a helpful way to nudge people into making healthier food choices.[70]

- Salience—People are more likely to choose options that are more noticeable than others. For example, one study found that snack shop consumers buy more fruit and healthy snacks when those options are placed right next to the cash register.[71]

The beauty of nudging is that it allows you to make smarter decisions and take better actions without even thinking about them. You simply shape your environment and then let your environment shape your decisions. Here are some examples of how you can use this strategy in your life:

- If you want to start flossing, put pre-made flossers in a cup next to your toothbrush.

- If you want to practice the guitar more often, place your guitar stand next to your living room couch.

- If you want to lose weight, store away your big plates and serve yourself on salad plates instead.

- If you want to read more, put a great book right on top of your favorite pillow.

- If you want to be more productive, use an app like Freedom to block distracting websites.

We tend to assume that good decisions require conscious effort, and that healthy behaviors require strong willpower. But often, all you need is a slight nudge in the right direction, and the rest will take care of itself. So take a look at your environment and ask yourself, "How can I make good choices easy and bad choices difficult?"

16. Conformity

*Matching attitudes, beliefs, and behaviors
to the norms of the group.*

In the 1950s, psychologist Solomon Asch conducted a series of experiments to investigate the power of social pressure.[72] At the start of each experiment, a participant entered a room with a group of strangers. The subject didn't know it, but these people were actors pretending to play the other participants.

The group was then given a simple task. First, they were shown a card with a single line on it and a second card with a series of lines. Each person was asked to point out the line on the second card that was the same length as the line on the first card.

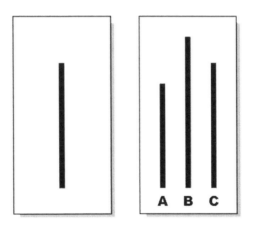

Initially, there were some easy trials where the entire group agreed on the same line. But after a few rounds, the actors would deliberately select what was obviously an incorrect answer. The bewildered subject then had to decide whether to trust their own judgment or conform to the group.

Asch ran this experiment several times in many different ways. And what he found was that as he increased the number of actors, the conformity of the subject also increased. One or two other "participants" had little impact. But as the number of actors increased to three, four, and all the way up to eight, the subject became more likely to give the same answer as everyone else.

Overall, 75 percent of participants gave an incorrect answer at least once. In the control group, where there was no pressure to conform to actors, the same error rate was less than 1 percent.

How could that be? Well, human beings are social creatures with a deep need for belonging. The reward of being accepted is usually greater than the reward of being accurate. So, for the most part, we'd rather be wrong in a group than right by ourselves.

As a species, we are ill-equipped to live on our own, so the human mind has evolved to get along with others. Because of that, we experience tremendous internal pressure to comply with the norms of the group. And, as a result, we tend to conform to those around us.

It's a natural thing to do, and there's nothing inherently wrong with it. But there can be severe downsides to this tendency. If you're not mindful of it, your intentions can get consistently overpowered by the prevailing group norms.

Consider, for instance, sleeping habits. Insufficient sleep ruins your health, performance, and well-being. Still, at least 50 percent of American adults are chronically sleep-deprived. And this devastating trend of sleeping too little is taking place throughout the industrialized world.[73]

There's a prevailing norm that sleep is a luxury rather than a necessity. And as the surrounding people conform to it, you'll likely do it, too.

If something seems like the normal thing to do, you'll naturally gravitate toward it—regardless of the outcome.

So make sure to surround yourself with people who consistently make the choices you want to make. Soon, the way they do things will become the way you do things.

17. Evolution by Natural Selection

The organisms best adapted to their environment tend to thrive.

In the nineteenth century, Charles Darwin and Alfred Russel Wallace ·
simultaneously had what's been called "the greatest idea anyone ever
had." They both independently realized that species evolve through
random mutation and differential survival rates.

Those best suited for survival in their environment tend to be
preserved. This process, where Mother Nature decides the success or
failure of particular mutations, is called "natural selection."[74]

To understand how it works, imagine a population of red beetles
living in a garden. Birds can spot and eat them pretty easily. But one
day, a random mutation—a small change in genetic instructions—
occurs, and a green baby beetle is born.

Purely by chance, the green beetle is nearly impossible for the birds
to see. Thanks to its accidental camouflage, it can survive, reproduce,
and pass on its genes more easily than the red beetles.

As a result, the green color becomes increasingly common in the
population. And if this process continues, eventually, all the beetles
in the garden will be green.

After reading Charles Darwin's *The Origin of Species*, English philosopher Herbert Spencer used the term "survival of the fittest" to
describe natural selection. This expression is still widely used today
and often misunderstood.

Many people think "fittest" means the best physical specimen of the
species and that only those in the best shape will survive in nature.

But that's not always the case. "Fittest," in this context, simply means the one best suited for the immediate environment.

And that idea applies in many other areas outside biology. Businesses, for example, are subject to their own kind of evolutionary arms races. To survive, a company constantly needs to adapt to an ever-evolving world and continually changing marketplace.

The video rental industry provides a great illustration of that. When Netflix launched in 1997, Blockbuster was the undisputed champion of their field. Between 1985 and 1992, the brick-and-mortar rental chain had expanded from its first location in Dallas, Texas, to over 2,800 locations around the world.

By the time Netflix came along with their rental-by-mail service, it looked like a classic David versus Goliath scenario. Still, they upended the video rental industry from day one. They had no late fees or shipping charges. If you lost a DVD, you got a new one in the mail with no questions asked.

Blockbuster tried to follow suit, matching service for service, but it was too late. In 2010 they filed for bankruptcy. Meanwhile, Netflix is still evolving, having gone from sending DVDs by mail, to streaming of other's content, to now streaming of their own content.

Their ability to adapt quickly to the ever-changing needs and preferences of their customers makes Netflix the "fittest" in their industry. Much like the green beetle in the garden, they are the ones best suited for their environment.

Evolution by natural selection is useful to understand because it explains what it takes to survive and thrive. To be successful, you need to embrace change. You have to pay attention to the ever-changing environment and rapidly adapt to it. If you do that, you can gain a critical advantage that puts you way ahead of the competition.

18. Homeostasis

The tendency of a system to maintain internal stability.

What's the temperature where you are right now? Most likely, it's not precisely 98.6°F (37.0°C). Still, your body temperature is probably very close to that value.

In fact, if your core body temperature doesn't stay within a narrow range—from about 95°F (35.0°C) to 107°F (41.7°C)—the results can be dangerous or even deadly.

So, as you're reading this, every cell in your body and brain are working to maintain a sense of stability. Not just in your core body temperature but also in blood pressure, heart rate, pH balance, blood glucose levels, and many other factors critical to your survival.

This tendency to maintain internal stability—this resistance to change—is called homeostasis, and the human body is just one example of where it takes place. In his book *Mastery*, George Leonard writes:

> *"[Homeostasis] characterizes all self-regulating systems, from a bacterium to a frog to a human individual to a family to an organization to an entire culture—and it applies to psychological states and behavior as well as to physical functioning."[75]*

Psychologically, we maintain homeostasis through mental patterns like the status quo bias—our tendency to prefer that things stay as they already are. Socially, we remain stable through forces like conformity—our propensity to maintain attitudes, beliefs, and behaviors congruent with the group.

Imagine, as an example, that for the last ten years or so, you've been almost entirely sedentary. But then, one day, you decide to go for a run. The first few steps are enjoyable, but that quickly changes. After a couple of minutes, you feel light-headed. Moments later, you feel sick to your stomach. And if you keep going, soon enough, you'll feel like if you don't stop, you might just drop dead.

These symptoms are essentially homeostatic alarm signals. Your body has detected changes in respiration, heart rate, and metabolism that are way outside the normal range. To bring them back, your body screams at you: *"Warning! Warning! Whatever you're doing, stop it immediately, or you're going to die!"*

And that's just one way that homeostasis gets in the way of your new fitness goal. On a psychological level, you'll probably experience resistance every time you think about putting on your running shoes. And on a social level, your sedentary friends might not welcome your new exercise habit.

Needless to say, homeostasis makes it difficult to create change. It's a powerful force that often results in backsliding. But the good news is that if you keep pushing, homeostasis will eventually adapt to the new load and create a new set point.

If you keep showing up at the trail, your body will eventually get used to the running, and even begin to crave it. Being a runner will become part of your self-image, and you'll experience resistance if you *don't* go running. And, with time, your friends will get used to this crazy habit of yours—and some of them might even join you.

So whenever you make a decision that requires a big change, expect homeostasis to kick in. Know that there will be backsliding and keep on pushing. Eventually, homeostasis will adapt and start working for you. And from that point forward, it will be much easier.

19. Fight or Flight

The instinctive physiological response to a threatening situation.

Imagine that you're a member of a nomadic tribe of hunter-gatherers living somewhere in North America during the Ice Age. You're out pursuing a bison when, suddenly, a sabre-tooth tiger jumps out in front of you.

At the sight of this threatening environmental stimulus, your body immediately launches into what's called the fight-or-flight response. Stress hormones flood the body and create physiological changes like:[76]

- Increased blood flow to activated muscles by diverting blood from other parts of the body.

- Higher blood pressure, heart rate, blood sugars, and fats to supply the body with a boost of energy.

- Faster blood clotting function to prevent excessive blood loss in case of injury.

- Greater muscle tension to provide the body with extra speed and strength.

These changes help you attack quickly or run like crazy. And if you're standing face-to-face with a sabre-tooth tiger, that's a very helpful reaction. The fight-or-flight response helped our ancestors stay alive, so we inherited it from them.

And while it's still useful, it can also be problematic. Our bodies don't distinguish well between threats to our survival and everyday stressors. So an angry boss, a challenging deadline, or an overwhelming workload can all set off the fight-or-flight response.

And when that happens, your ability to think is also affected. During the fight-or-flight response, your brain has increased activity in areas like the limbic system, which is associated with emotions. Meanwhile, it has decreased activity in areas like the prefrontal cortex, which is associated with decision-making.[77]

In the terms of Daniel Kahneman, you switch from the reflective System 2 to the reflexive System 1. And, as we've covered in a previous chapter, that means you become more susceptible to cognitive biases and logical fallacies. As a result, you're more likely to make hasty decisions based on habitual responses rather than deep thinking.

To be a good decision-maker, you need to be able to face the inevitable stressors of life without getting swept away by the fight-or-flight response. And the best way to do that is to proactively build your stress resilience and deliberately calm down before making important decisions.

Look after your most basic self-care needs. Get sufficient sleep, eat healthy foods, and be physically active every day. That will give your body and brain the rest, fuel, and outlet it needs to cope with the stress that it's experiencing. Prepare well and you'll perform well.

And whenever a big decision arises, take the time to breathe deeply, slow down, and concentrate. Make sure to switch from System 1 to System 2. Then use your mental model checklist to consider what's in front of you from different perspectives.

The less stressed you are, the clearer you'll think, and the better decisions you'll make.

20. Entropy

The tendency of everything to move from order to disorder.

The second law of thermodynamics states that "as one goes forward in time, the net entropy (degree of disorder) of any isolated or closed system will always increase (or at least stay the same)."[78]

That's basically a long way of saying that all things tend to move from order to disorder. This is one of the fundamental laws of the universe, and you can see its effects everywhere.

As a simple example, imagine that you walk into a café and order a cup of coffee. Normally, we don't think twice about a simple cup of coffee, but there's actually a lot of time and effort that's gone into it.

The barista reaches for a cup he has cleaned and someone else has made. He then pours water that a power company has heated over coffee beans that got there due to the work of many people. Airplanes, ships, and trucks burned fuel to get them to the café, as well.

Once you get the cup of coffee in your hand, it's a highly ordered structure in the universe. Its entropy is low.

Now, instead of drinking it, imagine what would happen if you just let it sit on the table for 30 minutes. After a while it gets cold. The heat energy moves from the cup and out into the room. That's a gain in entropy.

If you leave the cup for several days, some of the water you paid for will evaporate. It will move from the cup and turn into water vapor in the room. That's another gain in entropy.

Let the cup sit for years, and the material it's made of will eventually break down and fall apart. This, too, is yet another gain in entropy.

It's the natural tendency of all things to lose order. Left to their own devices, everything will become less structured. Gardens get weeds. Cars rust. People age. Civilizations fall. Ancient ruins crumble. Even great mountains gradually erode and disappear.

And the same relentless force is present in all areas of your life. If you don't move your body, you'll lose muscle mass. If you don't answer your emails, your in-box will flood. If you don't nurture your relationships, they will eventually die out.

But the good news is that it's possible to fight back against entropy. The barista can clean the cup and get it ready for the next customer. And you can expend the energy needed to maintain order in your life. It's hard, but also meaningful, work. As psychologist Steven Pinker puts it:

> "*The Second Law of Thermodynamics defines the ultimate purpose of life, mind, and human striving: to deploy energy and information to fight back the tide of entropy and carve out refuges of beneficial order.*"[79]

Knowing that everything naturally moves from order to disorder, you can deliberately simplify your life. Let go of everything unimportant so you can spend your limited energy where it truly matters. Carefully choose the areas where you want to fight entropy and tend to them consistently.

Not only will it make you more focused and efficient, but also happier and more fulfilled.

21. Margin of Safety

The ability to withstand challenges that are greater than expected.

Imagine that you're an engineer building a bridge. You know that, on an average day, the bridge will need to support about 10,000 tons of traffic at any given time. Would you build it to withstand exactly that weight?

Hopefully, your answer is "no." What if your estimates or calculations are slightly off? What if the bridge gets heavier traffic than average on certain days? What if your building materials are weaker than expected?

To account for all that, you decide to build a bridge that comfortably supports 50,000 tons. In engineering terms, the additional 40,000 ton capacity is a "margin of safety." It's the ability of your bridge to withstand challenges greater than expected.[80]

And that principle is very useful, not just in construction and engineering, but in many areas of life. Let's have a look at some examples.

Time Management

If you're always running late, it's because you're living your life without a sufficient margin of safety. The planning fallacy makes you overoptimistic, and you perpetually overlook that life is full of unexpected delays. To overcome that tendency, you can add extra buffer time before each task in your schedule.

Strength Training

If you push yourself to lift as heavy as you possibly can in the gym, you're eliminating your margin of safety. By instead finishing each set with at least one more repetition in you, you can execute every lift with proper form and reduce the risk of injury.

Personal Finance

If you spend every dime you earn each month, you don't have a financial margin of safety. There's no protection for unexpected expenses. Conversely, if you can get by on 90 percent of your income, the remaining 10 percent can provide a helpful financial buffer.

Investing

If you buy a stock because you consider it slightly undervalued, your investment has a poor margin of safety. Predicting the future is extremely difficult, and that's why famous investors like Warren Buffett usually only buy stocks that are excessively underpriced.

Stress Management

If you don't take care of yourself, you won't have a buffer to deal with the inevitable stressors in life. Good habits like sufficient sleep, healthy eating, regular movement, and mindfulness practice provides an emotional margin of safety for unusually bad days.

All information contains some amount of error. The future is uncertain and, as we learned in the last chapter, entropy makes it ever more complicated. By using a margin of safety, you get a cushion that protects against incorrect estimates, unforeseen events, and plain bad luck.

Always account for the hidden errors. Always leave room for the unexpected. Always be stronger than you need to be. That will make you confident and unshakable—even when things get extraordinarily difficult.

22. Antifragility

The ability to benefit from stressors.

In his book *Antifragile*, statistician and philosopher Nassim Nicholas Taleb writes:

> *"Some things benefit from shocks; they thrive and grow when exposed to volatility, randomness, disorder, and stressors and love adventure, risk, and uncertainty. Yet, in spite of the ubiquity of the phenomenon, there is no word for the exact opposite of fragile. Let us call it antifragile."*[81]

Taleb makes the case that people, organizations, and systems can be described in one of three ways: fragile, resilient, or antifragile. To understand the difference between these categories, imagine three packages that are being sent in the mail:

- The first package says "Handle with care." If you're not careful, everything inside the box will break. It's fragile.

- The second package says "Robust." This box can take some hits before the contents inside break. It's resilient.

- The third package says "Handle roughly." The stuff in this one actually gets stronger if you kick it around. It's antifragile.

Here's the takeaway: You don't want to be fragile. At the very least, you want to be resilient. And ideally, you want to be antifragile. Let's look at some ways you can move from fragility to robustness to antifragility in your life:

Follow *Via Negativa*

According to Taleb, "The first step towards antifragility consists in first decreasing downside."[82] You can do that through *via negativa*, which is Latin for "the negative way." Instead of asking yourself what to add to your life, you invert the question and ask yourself what to remove. For example, get out of debt, stop eating junk food, and quit smoking.

Manage Your Stress Response

When a stressor shows up in your life, there are two ways you can perceive it: as a threat or as a challenge. These different views create very different thoughts, emotions, and behaviors.[83] A threat response makes you fragile, while a challenge response makes you antifragile. So, develop a "Bring it on!" mentality, and stress will strengthen you.

Practice Voluntary Discomfort

The Spartan warriors had a creed that stated, "He who sweats more in training bleeds less in war." You can prepare yourself for the battles of life by practicing voluntary hardship. Occasionally take cold showers, live on a tight budget, drink water only, and so on. Get comfortable being uncomfortable, and the inevitable blows of life won't be as devastating.

Create Redundancies

Nature is filled with redundancies. For example, animals have two lungs, two kidneys, and two testicles, even though one of each would do just fine. But since one in a pair of organs can become disabled through disease or trauma, it pays to have a spare. You can use the same strategy to decrease fragility of the systems in your life. Start an emergency fund, have a spare tire in your car, use an external hard drive to back up your work, and so on.

Use the Barbell Strategy

Taleb describes "the barbell strategy" as "a dual attitude of playing it safe in some areas and taking a lot of small risks in others, hence achieving antifragility."[84] For example, you can keep your day job while working on a side hustle at night. If your side hustle doesn't work out, you still have an income stream, but if it does work out, you might create a more fulfilling and profitable career.

Philosopher Friedrich Nietzsche once said, *"That which does not kill us, makes us stronger."* Set yourself up for antifragility, and you'll find that famous quote to be true.

23. Newton's Laws of Motion

Three laws of mechanics describing the motions of objects.

In 1687, Isaac Newton published his revolutionary book, *The Principia: Mathematical Principles of Natural Philosophy*,[85] in which he stated his three laws of motion.

The *Principia* formed the foundation of classical mechanics and is to this day considered one of the most important works in the history of science.

And, as we'll see in this chapter, Newton's laws of motion can be used as helpful models to create progress in our lives.

Let's have a look at the three laws and use my author career as a simple example for each one.

The First Law of Motion: *Objects in motion tend to stay in motion, and objects at rest tend to stay at rest.*

Whenever you're procrastinating on something, you're experiencing the pull of this law firsthand. Objects at rest tend to stay at rest.

Luckily, it works the other way around, too. If you just get started, you'll generally keep going. Objects in motion tend to stay in motion.

When I started writing, I was constantly fighting this law. I only wrote sporadically and, as a result, getting started was a continuous struggle.

It wasn't until I got a regular writing routine down that I could start to benefit from this law.

Over time, writing first thing in the morning has become second nature. My new homeostasis, if you will.

And you can do the same thing in any area where you'd like to make progress. Get moving, and you'll keep going.

> *The Second Law of Motion: F=ma. Force equals mass times acceleration.*

There is one important takeaway in the F=ma equation. The force, F, is a vector. Vectors have both magnitude (the amount of effort put in) and direction (where that effort is applied).

If you want an object to accelerate in a particular direction, the amount of effort *and* the direction of that effort will both affect the outcome.

So whenever you want to make progress, it's not just about how hard you work (magnitude), but also about where you apply that work (direction).

As a writer, it's not just the number of quality words I write every day (magnitude) that affects the results in my business.

My decisions about whether to work as a freelancer, ghostwriter, or author (direction) are equally important.

As we've learned in a previous chapter, everything we do has an opportunity cost, so make sure that all your hard work is applied in the most beneficial direction.

> *The Third Law of Motion: For every action, there is an equal and opposite reaction.*

Much like this law describes, your progress is a balance of opposing forces in your life.

There are supporting forces like energy, focus, and motivation. And there are opposing forces like fatigue, overwhelm, and discouragement.

Whenever you want to make more progress, you have two options: you can add supporting forces, or you can remove opposing forces.

As a writer, I've added supporting forces like my daily writing routine, a high-quality writing application, and regular contact with other authors. I've also removed opposing forces like email notifications, desktop clutter, and most social media accounts. As a result, the progress I want to make every day now comes much more easily.

Nudge yourself in the right direction, and your behavior will spontaneously adapt.

Whenever you want to create progress in your life, keep these ideas in mind. Get moving, and you'll keep going. Apply your hard work in the most beneficial direction. And modify the opposing forces in your life. Use Newton's laws of motion to your advantage, and they will naturally carry you forward.

24. Algorithms

Well-defined instructions to perform certain tasks.

In his book *Homo Deus*, historian Yuval Noah Harari writes:

> *'Algorithm' is arguably the single most important concept in our world. If we want to understand our life and our future, we should make every effort to understand what an algorithm is, and how algorithms are connected with emotions.*[86]

So, what is an algorithm? The dictionary defines it as "a process or set of rules to be followed in calculations or other problem-solving operations, especially by a computer."

If you've ever wondered how a Tesla can drive itself, the answer is algorithms—millions of them. But there are also more relatable everyday occurrences of algorithms. Each time you bake a cake, for example, the recipe you use is an algorithm.

And, as psychologists have found, you can also use algorithms to program yourself for better decision-making. Psychology professor Peter Gollwitzer refers to this strategy as if-then planning.[87] To use it, all you have to do is fill out this simple formula:

If [situation]–Then I will [behavior].

The beauty of if-then planning is that it forces you to turn vague intentions into clear algorithms.

"I want to eat healthier," becomes *"If I'm buying lunch, then I will order a salad."*

It sounds ridiculously simple, but don't let that fool you. Over 200 scientific studies show that if-then planners are about 300 percent more likely to achieve their goals. The reason it works so exceptionally well, according to psychologist Heidi Grant, is that "Contingencies are built into our neurological wiring. Humans are very good at encoding information in 'If X, then Y' terms, and using those connections (often unconsciously) to guide their behavior."[88]

In other words: much like computers, our minds respond very well to algorithms. If-then plans allow you to act the way you want without thinking, and that saves a lot of mental energy for other decisions. Instead of hesitating and deliberating, you just follow the algorithm whenever the situation arises. Here are some more examples:

- *"I want to move more."* → If I'm at work, then I will take the stairs.

- *"I want to be more productive."* → If I arrive at the office, then I will do two hours of deep work.

- *"I want to improve my relationships."* → If I come home from work, then I will share the best thing that happened to me that day.

- *"I want to be happier"* → If I wake up in the morning, then I will think about one thing I'm grateful for.

- *"I want to make better decisions."* → If I'm making an important decision, then I will review my checklist of mental models.

Instead of relying on vague intentions, purposely install the responses that will lead you to your goals. Think of yourself as a robot and the if-then plans as the algorithms you use to program yourself. It sounds silly, I know, but it's a remarkably effective way of putting good decisions on autopilot.

25. Compounding

Interest on interest.

Imagine that you're given a choice right now. You can get either $3 million in cash immediately, or a penny that doubles in value every day for the next 30 days. Which option would you choose?

Most people would take the $3 million. Let's say you do that, and I get the penny.

At the outset, you'll have every reason to be happy with your choice. After one week of compounding, my penny is worth a meager 64 cents. After two weeks, it's at a modest $81.92. And after three weeks, I'm still way behind you. Sure, the penny has transformed into a respectable $10,485.76, but that's still not much compared to your $3 million.

But then, a few days into the third week, the magic of compounding starts to show. On day 28, the penny has grown into a remarkable $1,342,177.28. On day 29, I'm right behind you with $2,684,354.56. And on day 30, I finally pull ahead as my stack of cash compounds into an astonishing $5,368,709.12.

DAY	VALUE	DAY	VALUE	DAY	VALUE
1	$0.01	11	$10.24	21	$10,485.76
2	$0.02	12	$20.48	22	$20,971.52
3	$0.04	13	$40.96	23	$41,943.04
4	$0.08	14	$81.92	24	$83,886.08
5	$0.16	15	$163.84	25	$167,772.16
6	$0.32	16	$327.68	26	$335,544.32
7	$0.64	17	$655.36	27	$671,088.64
8	$1.28	18	$1,310.72	28	$1,342,177.28
9	$2.56	19	$2,621.44	29	$2,684,354.56
10	$5.12	20	$5,242.88	30	$5,368,709.12

The compounding penny illustrates something that our brains have a hard time grasping intuitively: small improvements add up to massive changes over time. And this is just as true in life as in finance. In his book *Atomic Habits*, author James Clear explains:[89]

> *"Here's how the math works out: if you can get 1 percent better each day for one year, you'll end up thirty-seven times better by the time you're done. Conversely, if you get 1 percent worse each day for one year, you'll decline nearly down to zero. What starts as a small win or a minor setback accumulates into something much more. Habits are the compound interest of self-improvement."*

Whenever you make a mundane choice, like ordering a salad instead of a hamburger, that single occasion won't make much of a difference. But as you keep repeating the same decisions and actions over weeks, months, and years, they will compound into significant results.

- If you hit the gym for an hour three times a week, and you do this for a week, you won't get any noticeable results (except maybe some soreness). But if you keep showing up just as often for a year, you'll accumulate 156 hours of exercise. That's more than enough to have a significant effect on your health and fitness.

- If you read one good book, that won't make much of an impact on your thinking. But if you read one every month for a year, you'll finish twelve titles. That will equip your mind with plenty of new mental models to improve your thinking.

- If you meditate a couple of times, it probably won't create any lasting changes. But if you do it for 10 minutes each day for a year, you'll have 60+ hours of meditation practice. And that will most likely have considerable positive effects on your health, well-being, and performance.

There is immense power in tiny improvements. Instead of looking for big wins, start small. Focus on getting just one percent better every day. Allow compounding to work its magic and, over time, it will create remarkable outcomes.

PART 5: FINAL WORDS

The chief enemy of good decisions is a lack of sufficient perspectives on a problem.

—Alain de Botton

A Little Wiser Every Day

The British statistician George Box is considered to be one of the great statistical minds of the twentieth century.

In a groundbreaking 1976 paper, he wrote the famous line, "All models are wrong, some are useful."[90]

Box argued that, instead of endlessly debating whether a model is correct in every instance, we should apply it where it's helpful.

For a great illustration of this principle, let's consider the work of Albert Einstein.

All Ideas Are Imperfect

In 1915, Einstein published one of the most remarkable achievements in science to date: the general theory of relativity.[91]

This idea had a profound effect on our understanding of the universe, and the theory has held up remarkably well over the years.

For instance, general relativity predicted the existence of gravitational waves, ripples in space-time, which weren't directly observed until 2015—100 years after Einstein's prediction.

But even the most brilliant of ideas are imperfect. While general relativity explains how the universe works in many situations, it also breaks down in certain extreme scenarios like, inside black holes.

Utility Over Accuracy

According to historian Yuval Noah Harari, "Scientists usually assume that no theory is 100 percent correct. Consequently, truth is a poor test for knowledge. The real test is utility. A theory that enables us to do new things constitutes knowledge."[92]

Einstein's general theory of relativity doesn't work in every instance, but when it's applied in the right areas, it's incredibly useful.

Not only has it dramatically improved our understanding of the universe, but it's also been extremely valuable for practical, everyday purposes.

The GPS in your phone, for example, has to take the effects of relativity into account to give you accurate directions. If it wasn't for Einstein's imperfect idea, your navigation system wouldn't work.

A Framework for Effective Thinking

Just like the general theory of relativity, every idea presented in this book is imperfect. Our minds are puzzling, our decisions are complicated, and there are no "one size fits all" models to make sense of everything.

No cognitive bias explains all the ways our thinking goes wrong. No logical fallacy describes all the ways that our reasoning breaks down. And no mental model offers a perfect tool for every problem we come across.

But together, all of these concepts make up a useful framework for effective thinking. Combined, they provide a helpful understanding of how your cognitive apparatus works and how to use it.

The more you improve that framework, the more versatile and

accurate your thinking will become. And that will help you make ever smarter decisions that lead to increasingly better results.

Remove Your Blind Spots

As you approach problems and decisions, you will have certain blind spots. Sometimes, you'll fall victim to a cognitive bias or logical fallacy. Other times, you'll lack the appropriate mental model or use the wrong one.

Thinking is difficult. There is only one way to be rational, but many ways to be irrational. And since that's the case, you'll inevitably make mistakes from time to time.

Your goal shouldn't be to make perfect decisions every single time. That's not realistic, nor helpful. Instead, your goal should be to continually reduce your blind spots.

In other words, don't try to be intelligent; try not to be stupid.

Use The Decision-Making Blueprint Bonus Bundle to get a deep understanding of the concepts in this book. Put your framework solidly in place—and then continuously improve upon it.

Always Get Smarter

Anyone can improve their thinking, but most of us won't put in the effort. It's much easier and more immediately gratifying to zone out, watch TV, or browse social media.

But that won't help you accumulate useful knowledge, expand your mental toolbox, and make better decisions.

So as our journey together comes to an end, I'd like to leave you with the following piece of advice from Charlie Munger:

"Go to bed smarter than when you woke up."[93]

That simple principle will allow wisdom to build up, integrate, and compound at a remarkable rate.

Make a commitment to lifelong learning. Set aside a little time every day for self-education. Fuel your curiosity and seek to get a little bit wiser every day.

Piece by piece, you'll expand your mental framework. Day by day, you'll make better decisions. And little by little, you'll improve the results in all areas of your life.

Download Your Free Bonus Bundle

You've made it to the end of this book. Great job reading all the way through! If you're excited to put everything you've learned to use, I recommend you download your free copy of The Decision-Making Blueprint Bonus Bundle right now.

This companion resource will make it as easy as possible for you to internalize all the concepts covered in this book and use them in your decision-making.

Get Your Next Blueprint

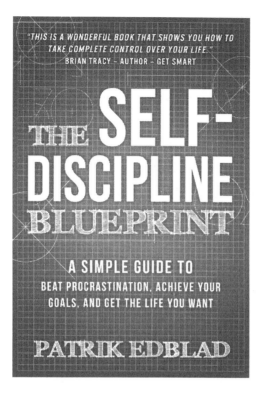

The Self-Discipline Blueprint is the complete step-by-step guide to achieving anything you set your mind to. Each chapter covers practical and efficient ways to develop relentless self-discipline, all backed by research. Inside the book, you'll discover:

- the four fundamental keystone habits of self-discipline;
- how to establish your mission in life using the Hedgehog Concept;
- how to find your unique "why" using the Golden Circle;
- how to biologically reshape your mind and body for success by creating a Winner Effect;
- and much more.

PLUS: The Self-Discipline Blueprint Workbook—a bonus resource you can use to put everything you learn into immediate action.

Take the next step in your self-actualization journey right now:

Go here to get the Self-Discipline Blueprint today!

http://PatrikEdblad.com/books/the-self-discipline-blueprint

Acknowledgments

I have relied on a lot of people while creating this book. Before anyone else, I want to thank my girlfriend Lisa who, as always, has provided invaluable guidance and encouragement at every step along the way. Second, I'm deeply grateful for the unceasing support of my family, friends, and peers. And third, to all my wonderful readers for their continuous feedback and supportive messages.

As for the content of the book, I have a long list of brilliant thinkers, educators, and researchers to thank. Daniel Kahneman, Amos Tversky, Dan Ariely, Charlie Munger, Shane Parrish, James Clear, Derek Muller, Gabriel Weinberg, Buster Benson, Bo Bennett, and Kevin deLaplante have all deeply influenced my understanding of decision-making. If you enjoyed this book, I highly recommend you check out their work as well.

To Kristie, Rob, Jordan, Erica, Vanessa, and the rest of the fabulous team at Archangel Ink, thank you for another great collaboration and for making this book a reality. I'm also grateful to the talented Sarah Moore, who designed the beautiful images in this book.

I'm sure there are people I've forgotten, but I keep an updated list of anyone who's influenced my work in meaningful ways at patrikedblad.com/thanks.

And finally, to you. Life is short and there are countless books to choose from. Thank you for sharing some of your precious time with me by reading this book. I hope you found it insightful.

Endnotes

1. "Prospect Theory: An Analysis of Decision under Risk." Jstor. Accessed July 30, 2019. https://www.jstor.org/stable/1914185.

2. "Half of U.S. Adults Would Change at Least One Education Decision." Gallup. Accessed July 30, 2019. https://news.gallup.com/poll /211529/half-adults-change-least-one-education-decision.aspx.

3. "1 in 3 adults don't get enough sleep." CDC Online Newsroom, CDC. Accessed July 30, 2019. https://www.cdc.gov/media/releases/2016/p0215 -enough-sleep.html.

4. "Physical Inactivity: A Global Public Health Problem." WHO. Accessed July 30, 2019. https://www.who.int/dietphysicalactivity/factshe et_inactivity/en/.

5. "Health effects of dietary risks in 195 ...." Lancet. Accessed July 30, 2019. https://www.thelancet.com/article/S0140-6736(19)30041-8/full text.

6. "Marriage and Divorce - American ...." APA. Accessed July 30, 2019. https://www.apa.org/topics/divorce/.

7. *The Top Five Regrets of the Dying: A Life Transformed by the Dearly Departing* by Bronnie Ware: https://www.goodreads.com/book/show/130 59271-the-top-five-regrets-of-the-dying

8. "Largest neuronal network simulation achieved using K computer ...." Riken. Accessed July 30, 2019. http://www.riken.jp/en/pr/press/2013/20 130802_1/.

9. "(PDF) The Evolution of Cognitive Bias." ResearchGate. Accessed July 30, 2019. https://www.researchgate.net/publication/308584925_The _Evolution_of_Cognitive_Bias.

10. "(PDF) Medicine. Do defaults save lives?" ResearchGate. Accessed July 30, 2019. https://www.researchgate.net/publication/8996952_Medicine_Do_defaults_save_lives.

11. "(PDF) On the Failure to Eliminate Hypotheses in a Conceptual Task." Accessed July 30, 2019. https://pdfs.semanticscholar.org/86db/64c600fe59acfc48fd22bc8484485d5e7337.pdf.

12. "Self-serving bias in the classroom: Who shows it? Who knows it?" Accessed July 30, 2019. https://psycnet.apa.org/record/1996-01721-010.

13. "Explanations for unemployment in Britain." Wiley Online Library. Accessed July 30, 2019. https://onlinelibrary.wiley.com/doi/pdf/10.1002/ejsp.2420120402.

14. "(PDF) Attributions in the Sports Pages - ResearchGate." Accessed July 30, 2019. https://www.researchgate.net/publication/232567890_Attributions_in_the_Sports_Pages.

15. *The Better Angels of Our Nature: Why Violence Has Declined* by Steven Pinker: https://www.goodreads.com/book/show/13543093-the-better-angels-of-our-nature

16. *Thinking, Fast and Slow* by Daniel Kahneman, page 8: https://www.goodreads.com/book/show/12385458-thinking-fast-and-slow

17. "Abraham Wald's Work on Aircraft Survivability." ResearchGate. Accessed July 30, 2019. https://www.researchgate.net/publication/254286514_Abraham_Wald's_Work_on_Aircraft_Survivability.

18. Daniel Kahneman: The Trouble with Confidence: https://www.youtube.com/watch?v=tyDQFmA1SpU

19. "The Endowment Effect, Loss Aversion, and Status Quo Bias." ResearchGate. Accessed July 30, 2019. https://www.researchgate.net/profile/Richard_Thaler/publication/4730791_The_Endowment_Effect_Loss_Aversion_and_Status_Quo_Bias/links/09e4151030d3ea82e9000000/The-Endowment-Effect-Loss-Aversion-and-Status-Quo-Bias.pdf.

20. "Status Quo Bias in Decision Making." Accessed October 21, 2019. https://sites.hks.harvard.edu/fs/rzeckhau/status%20quo%20bias.pdf.

21. "(PDF) Medicine. Do defaults save lives?" ResearchGate. Accessed July 30, 2019. https://www.researchgate.net/publication/8996952_Medicine_Do_defaults_save_lives.

22. "Anchoring bias in decision-making." ScienceDaily. Accessed July 30, 2019. https://www.sciencedaily.com/terms/anchoring.htm.

23. "Models of Temporal Discounting 1937–2000: An Interdisciplinary ...." Accessed July 30, 2019. https://people.kth.se/~gryne/papers/Hyperbol_150401.pdf.

24. "Time Discounting and Time Preference: A Critical Review." Universitat Innsbruck. Accessed July 30, 2019. https://www.uibk.ac.at/economics/bbl/lit_se/lit_se_ss06_papiere/time_discounting.pdf.

25. "I'll have the ice cream soon and the vegetables later: A ..." Springer. Accessed July 30, 2019. https://link.springer.com/article/10.1007/s11002-009-9087-0.

26. *The Marshmallow Test: Mastering Self-Control* by Walter Mischel: https://www.goodreads.com/book/show/20454074-the-marshmallow-test

27. "Unskilled and Unaware of It: How Difficulties in ..." Semantic Scholar. Accessed July 30, 2019. https://pdfs.semanticscholar.org/e320/9ca64cbed9a441e55568797cbd3683cf7f8c.pdf.

28. "The Anosognosic's Dilemma." Opinionator - The New York Times. Accessed July 30, 2019. https://opinionator.blogs.nytimes.com/2010/06/20/the-anosognosics-dilemma-1/.

29. "Everyone has a bias blind spot, researchers find." ScienceDaily. Accessed July 30, 2019. https://www.sciencedaily.com/releases/2015/06/150608213028.htm.

30. "Bias Blind Spot: Structure, Measurement, and ..." ResearchGate. Accessed July 30, 2019. https://www.researchgate.net/publication/275723 267_Bias_Blind_Spot_Structure_Measurement_and_Consequences.

31. *Elementary Lessons in Logic: Deductive and Inductive: With Copious Questions and Examples, and a Vocabulary of Logical Terms* by William Stanley Jevons, page 169: https://www.goodreads.com/book/show/21852 80.Elementary_Lessons_In_Logic

32. "(PDF) Medicine. Do defaults save lives?" ResearchGate. Accessed July 30, 2019. https://www.researchgate.net/publication/8996952_Medic ine_Do_defaults_save_lives.

33. "Law Of Large Numbers: Overview." Investopedia. Accessed July 30, 2019. https://www.investopedia.com/terms/l/lawoflargenumbers.asp.

34. *Thinking, Fast and Slow* by Daniel Kahneman, page 113: https://www .goodreads.com/book/show/12385458-thinking-fast-and-slow

35. "Correlation does not imply causation." Semantic Scholar. Accessed July 30, 2019. https://pdfs.semanticscholar.org/d886/674ab022d6d34447 320ed62b96ebab9ead60.pdf.

36. *Spurious Correlations* by Tyler Vigen: https://www.goodreads.com/bo ok/show/23197309-spurious-correlations

37. Full Service Moving Commercial from United Van Lines: https:// www.youtube.com/watch?v=_DMUGabJ8Mw

38. "The psychology of sunk cost." ResearchGate. Accessed July 30, 2019. https://www.researchgate.net/publication/4812596_The_psychology_of _sunk_cost.

39. "It's About Time: Optimistic Predictions in Work and Love." Taylor&Francis Online. Accessed July 30, 2019. https://www.tandfonline .com/doi/pdf/10.1080/14792779343000112.

40. "DENVER INTERNATIONAL AIRPORT Information on ..."
GovInfo. Accessed July 30, 2019. https://www.govinfo.gov/content/pkg
/GAOREPORTS-AIMD-95-230/pdf/GAOREPORTS-AIMD-95
-230.pdf.

41. "The Hourglass Is Half Full or Half Empty: Temporal ..." APA
PsycNET. Accessed July 30, 2019. https://psycnet.apa.org/record/2005
-11262-003.

42. "The Hourglass Is Half Full or Half Empty: Temporal ..." APA
PsycNET. Accessed July 30, 2019. https://psycnet.apa.org/record/2005
-11262-003.

43. "People focus on optimistic scenarios and disregard ..." ResearchGate.
Accessed July 30, 2019. https://www.researchgate.net/publication/123097
70_People_focus_on_optimistic_scenarios_and_disregard_pessimistic_sc
enarios_when_predicting_task_completion_times.

44. "Fallacy fallacy." RationalWiki. Accessed July 30, 2019. https://
rationalwiki.org/wiki/Fallacy_fallacy.

45. *Behave: The Biology of Humans at Our Best and Worst* by Robert M.
Sapolsky, page 5: https://www.goodreads.com/book/show/31170723-be
have

46. *Thinking, Fast and Slow* by Daniel Kahneman, page 20: https://www
.goodreads.com/book/show/12385458-thinking-fast-and-slow

47. *Thinking, Fast and Slow* by Daniel Kahneman, page 28: https://www
.goodreads.com/book/show/12385458-thinking-fast-and-slow

48. "A Non-Aristotelian System and its Necessity for Rigour in
Mathematics and Physics." Accessed July 30, 2019. http://esgs.free.fr/uk
/art/sands-sup3.pdf.

49. "The Map Is Not the Territory." Farnam Street." Accessed July 30,
2019. https://fs.blog/2015/11/map-and-territory/.

50. "Cours d'Économie Politique." SAGE Journals. Accessed July 30, 2019. http://journals.sagepub.com/doi/abs/10.1177/000271629700900314.

51. *Manual of Political Economy: A Critical and Variorum Edition* by Vilfredo Pareto: https://www.goodreads.com/book/show/22123853-manual-of-political-economy

52. "Chairman's Letter – 1996." Berkshire Hathaway Inc. Accessed July 30, 2019. https://www.berkshirehathaway.com/letters/1996.html.

53. "Understanding your Circle of Competence: How Warren Buffett Avoids ...." Farnam Street. Accessed July 30, 2019. https://fs.blog/2013/12/circle-of-competence/.

54. "The Four Burners Theory: The Downside of Work-Life ...." James Clear. Accessed July 30, 2019. https://jamesclear.com/four-burners-theory.

55. *Principles of Economics* by N. Gregory Mankiw, page 4: https://www.goodreads.com/book/show/5754642-principles-of-economics

56. "Introducing the Eisenhower Matrix." Accessed July 30, 2019. https://www.eisenhower.me/eisenhower-matrix/.

57. "Elon Musk's Mission to Mars." WIRED. Accessed July 30, 2019. https://www.wired.com/2012/10/ff-elon-musk-qa/.

58. "Elon Musk says he owes his success to a 3-step problem-solving trick ...." Business Insider. Accessed July 30, 2019. https://www.businessinsider.in/elon-musk-says-he-owes-his-success-to-a-3-step-problem-solving-trick-also-used-by-thomas-edison-and-nikola-tesla/articleshow/68515173.cms.

59. *The Most Important Thing: Uncommon Sense for the Thoughtful Investor* by Howard Marks, page 4: https://www.goodreads.com/book/show/10454418-the-most-important-thing

60. "Cane Toad." National Geographic. Accessed July 30, 2019. https://www.nationalgeographic.com/animals/amphibians/c/cane-toad/.

61. *The Most Important Thing: Uncommon Sense for the Thoughtful Investor* by Howard Marks, page 4: https://www.goodreads.com/book/show/1045 4418-the-most-important-thing

62. "Carl Gustav Jacob Jacobi." Wikipedia. Accessed July 30, 2019. https://en.wikipedia.org/wiki/Carl_Gustav_Jacob_Jacobi.

63. "Bayes' theorem." Wikipedia. Accessed July 30, 2019. https://en.wiki pedia.org/wiki/Bayes%27_theorem.

64. "The legend of Len Bias." ESPN.com. Accessed July 30, 2019. https://www.espn.com/espn/page2/story?page=jackson/060619_bias.

65. "What is Occam's Razor?" UCR Math. Accessed July 30, 2019. http://math.ucr.edu/home/baez/physics/General/occam.html.

66. "Of Rats, Rice, and Race: The Great Hanoi Rat Massacre, an Episode in French Colonial History." Freakonomics. Accessed July 30, 2019. http://www.freakonomics.com/media/vannrathunt.pdf.

67. "Operant conditioning." Wikipedia. Accessed July 30, 2019. https://en.wikipedia.org/wiki/Operant_conditioning.

68. *Nudge: Improving Decisions About Health, Wealth, and Happiness* by Richard H. Thaler, Cass R. Sunstein, page 4: https://www.goodreads.com/book/show/6359469-nudge

69. "Green defaults: Information presentation and pro ..." ScienceDirect.com. Accessed July 30, 2019. https://www.sciencedirect.com/science/artic le/abs/pii/S0272494407000758.

70. "The Hunger Games: Using hunger to promote ..." ScienceDirect.com. Accessed July 30, 2019. https://www.sciencedirect.com/science/artic le/pii/S0195666316308029.

71. "Nudging healthy food choices: a field experiment at the train ..." NCBI. Accessed July 30, 2019. https://www.ncbi.nlm.nih.gov/pubmed /26186924.

72. "Effects of group pressure upon the modification and ..." APA PsycNET. Accessed July 30, 2019. https://psycnet.apa.org/record/1952 -00803-001.

73. *Power Sleep: The Revolutionary Program That Prepares Your Mind for Peak Performance* by James B. Maas, page 16: https://www.goodreads.com /book/show/259777.Power_Sleep

74. "Natural selection." Understanding Evolution. Accessed July 30, 2019. https://evolution.berkeley.edu/evolibrary/article/evo_25.

75. *Mastery: The Keys to Success and Long-Term Fulfillment* by George Leonard, page 108: https://www.goodreads.com/book/show/18340786 -mastery

76. "Fight-or-flight response: Function of physiological changes." Wikipedia. Accessed July 30, 2019. https://en.wikipedia.org/wiki/Fight -or-flight_response.

77. "Stress potentiates decision biases: A stress ..." ScienceDirect.com. Accessed July 30, 2019. https://www.sciencedirect.com/science/article/pii /S2352289515300187.

78. "The Arrow of Time." Exactly What Is Time? Accessed July 30, 2019. http://www.exactlywhatistime.com/physics-of-time/the-arrow-of -time/.

79. "The Second Law of Thermodynamics." Edge.org. Accessed July 30, 2019. https://www.edge.org/response-detail/27023.

80. "Margin of Safety Definition and Examples used in Safety ..." OSTI. gov. Accessed July 30, 2019. https://www.osti.gov/servlets/purl/1134068.

81. *Antifragile: Things That Gain from Disorder* by Nassim Nicholas Taleb, page 3: https://www.goodreads.com/book/show/13530973-antifragile

82. *Antifragile: Things That Gain from Disorder* by Nassim Nicholas Taleb, page 159: https://www.goodreads.com/book/show/13530973-antifragile

83. "Threat and challenge: cognitive appraisal and stress ..." Academia. edu. Accessed July 30, 2019. https://www.academia.edu/11973248/Thre at_and_challenge_cognitive_appraisal_and_stress_responses_in_simula ted_trauma_resuscitations.

84. *Antifragile: Things That Gain from Disorder* by Nassim Nicholas Taleb, page 161: https://www.goodreads.com/book/show/13530973-antifragile

85. *The Principia: Mathematical Principles of Natural Philosophy* by Isaac Newton: https://www.goodreads.com/book/show/231083.The_Principia

86. *Homo Deus: A History of Tomorrow* by Yuval Noah Harari, page 83: https://www.goodreads.com/book/show/31138556-homo-deus

87. "Implementation Intentions and Effective Goal Pursuit." ResearchGate. Accessed July 30, 2019. https://www.researchgate.net /publication/37367645_Implementation_Intentions_and_Effective_Go al_Pursuit.

88. "Get Your Team to Do What It Says It's Going to Do." HBR. Accessed July 30, 2019. https://hbr.org/2014/05/get-your-team-to-do -what-it-says-its-going-to-do.

89. *Atomic Habits: An Easy & Proven Way to Build Good Habits & Break Bad Ones* by James Clear, page 15: https://www.goodreads.com/book/sh ow/40244063-atomic-habits

90. "Science and Statistics." Journal of the American Statistical Association. Accessed July 30, 2019. http://mkweb.bcgsc.ca/pointsofsigni ficance/img/Boxonmaths.pdf.

91. "The General Theory of Relativity." Accessed July 30, 2019. http://ion trap.umd.edu/wp-content/uploads/2016/01/WudkaGR-7.pdf.

92. *Sapiens: A Brief History of Humankind* by Yuval Noah Harari, page 288: https://www.goodreads.com/book/show/23198201-sapiens

93. "The Buffett Formula: Going to Bed Smarter Than When You Woke Up." Farnam Street. Accessed July 30, 2019. https://fs.blog/2013/05/the -buffett-formula/.

Made in the USA
Columbia, SC
14 March 2022

57622751R00089